WHEN THE PENNY DROPS

When the Penny Drops
Learning What's Not Taught

R. GOPALAKRISHNAN

Foreword by
ARUN MAIRA

PORTFOLIO
PENGUIN

PORTFOLIO
Published by the Penguin Group
Penguin Books India Pvt. Ltd, 11 Community Centre, Panchsheel Park,
New Delhi 110 017, India
Penguin Group (USA) Inc., 375 Hudson Street, New York, New York 10014,
USA
Penguin Group (Canada), 90 Eglinton Avenue East, Suite 700, Toronto,
Ontario, M4P 2Y3, Canada (a division of Pearson Penguin Canada Inc.)
Penguin Books Ltd, 80 Strand, London WC2R 0RL, England
Penguin Ireland, 25 St. Stephen's Green, Dublin 2, Ireland (a division of
Penguin Books Ltd)
Penguin Group (Australia), 250 Camberwell Road, Camberwell, Victoria
3124, Australia (a division of Pearson Australia Group Pty Ltd)
Penguin Group (NZ), 67 Apollo Drive, Rosedale, North Shore 0632, New
Zealand (a division of Pearson New Zealand Ltd)
Penguin Group (South Africa) (Pty) Ltd, 24 Sturdee Avenue, Rosebank,
Johannesburg 2196, South Africa

Penguin Books Ltd, Registered Offices: 80 Strand, London WC2R 0RL, England

First published in Portfolio by Penguin Books India 2010

Copyright © R. Gopalakrishnan 2010
Foreword copyright © Arun Maira 2010

All rights reserved

10 9 8 7 6 5 4 3 2 1

ISBN 9780670082964

Typeset in Minion by Eleven Arts, Keshav Puram, Delhi
Printed at Manipal Press Ltd, Manipal

**Dedicated to the memory of the late Tarun Sheth who shared so much with me
about personal development and careers**

Contents

Foreword

A common joke about consultants is they borrow a client's watch to tell the client the time. One may wonder why the client could not have looked at the watch himself to discover the time. We need 'insights' into ourselves, as much as we need insights into the world around us. The latter can be explained to us by good teachers and clever consultants. The former must be self-realized. Why do we need another to help us discover something that is within us? To see ourselves we need a mirror. Great consultants and great teachers hold up clear mirrors before us. They make us look into them and see ourselves. This is the concept of the Clementine Mirror which R. Gopalakrishnan explains in his book *When the Penny Drops.* He has written a book designed to make the reader reflect on himself.

In a scene from a very old movie, a young Mae West, who later grows into one of the greatest stars of her time, is auditioned by an agent. She performs many song and dance routines with great flourish to impress him. The agent asks her where she learned them. She says that she watches all the best shows and works hard to copy the routines. 'I thought so,' says the agent. Then he asks her, 'What do you want to be?' She replies, 'I want to be a star.' 'Then look into yourself,' he says. 'Stars are not a combination of others' tricks. They are special. They are one of a kind.' Similarly, leaders are not made: leaders become. But people want the easy way out. They want to know the six, seven or eight tricks of becoming a leader—rather, to being seen as a leader. There are dozens of best-selling books offering such tips. Fortunately, *When the Penny Drops* is not one of them.

In his essay 'Borges and I', the great writer Jorge Luis Borges wonders who he is. He says, 'The other one, the one called Borges, is the one things happen to. I know of Borges from the mail and see his name on a list of professors or in a biographical dictionary. I like hourglasses, maps, eighteenth century typography, the taste of coffee and the prose of Stevenson; he shares these preferences, but in a vain way that turns them into the attributes of an actor.' Borges ends his very brief essay—it is only one paragraph, with the thought, 'I do not know which of us has written this page.' I have read Borges's short piece many times over the years. It provokes me to think about myself: who is reading the page—Arun Maira or I? In the same vein, R. Gopalakrishnan's book wants you to think of yourself, of why you do what you do, and who you are.

His is not a book about famous people with lessons that one is supposed to learn from their remarkable stories. This is a book about regular people, including unsuccessful managers. It is a book with anecdotes that many people may relate to as the sort of things that happen to them and people around them all the time. Thus they can see themselves in these stories.

I set the book down many times as I read it. Because it triggered reflections on events in my own life. I know that it is not easy to write such a book. When I set down to write my first book, *The Accelerating Organization: Embracing the Human Face of Change*, the publisher wanted me to write an 'accessible' book for managers. Ken Blanchard's *The One Minute Manager* had broken sales records for a management book. The publisher gave me a copy. He wanted me to present my ideas in a similar style. It was not easy and I never quite made it. However I thought I had something important to say. I asked my friend Peter Senge, author of *The Fifth Discipline*, a seminal book about 'learning organizations', to review my book and consider writing a foreword for it. *The Fifth Discipline*, a profound book, had been a best-seller some years earlier. It visibly adorned the bookshelves of many managers, most of whom had not read it. 'The least read management best-seller ever,' Peter would joke. Peter read my manuscript. He said it was a good book and he endorsed the ideas in it. However, he said he could not bring himself to write the foreword. He said I was trying to pander to lazy business managers who wanted to be spoon-fed and given advice in 'sound-bites' and 'elevator talks'. He did not want to encourage this trend.

Warren Bennis and my friend and former colleague Robert Thomas (whose works Gopalakrishnan also refers to) observed in their book, *Geeks and Geezers*, that leaders come in many shapes and act in many different ways. Leaders are distinguishable as leaders because of what they accomplish and not by any externally observable, common set of habits. Bennis and Thomas's analysis of how leaders become leaders points to tough situations in their lives that shaped them. They say that such situations are not uncommon, and that many people find themselves in similar situations. However, people respond differently. Those who do not see themselves as merely helpless victims, but examine their own responses and take charge of their own transformation can develop the tough material of leadership within themselves. Thus these authors develop the concept of the crucible of leadership. The crucible is a container within which, by a transformative process, base metal may become noble. Their insight is that the crucible is not just the external situation. It is also the response within the person.

The dropping of the penny is an external event. Trapped by listening and learning disabilities, or bonsai traps as Gopalakrishnan calls them, we often do not hear the penny drop. But when the mind is open, the penny drop can trigger precious insights into oneself. In the variety of situations that Gopalakrishnan describes in his book, readers may find some that trigger such insights. An even greater gain from reading the book would be the recognition by readers of their own learning disabilities, or bonsai traps, and thereby a greater openness to learn and to know who they are.

Arun Maira
Member, Planning Commission,
Government of India

Preface

Recently I began the forty-fourth year of my management career. As a matter of course, I reflect on the valuable lessons that I have learned on my journey. I often meet peers who have had similar experiences as I, both in quality and in years. They too share with me the lessons that they have learned.

The common feature of the lessons that we all recall is that they are not easy to teach. The lessons are self-learned from personal experience or from others' stories. All of us feel that when the experience is narrated to someone else, that person may relate to it, musing, 'I have been down that road myself.' When you recognize your own thoughts and feelings in someone else's story, it creates an opportunity for reflection and learning.

How does reflection, which is prompted by your own or another's experience, help you learn? It does so by shaping your learning agenda. According to Robert Thomas, an influential thinker on this subject, you learn from experiences when you are able to see a connection among three things:[1]

* *Aspirations:* your personal aspirations or what you think is your ideal self
* *Motivations:* your deepest motivations or what you most deeply value
* *Learning:* learning style or how you as a person learn most effectively

Your aspirations, motivations and learning style strongly influence what you learn and from where. In simple words, you must want to learn. I have been inspired by the sayings of Swami Vivekananda, the great nineteenth-century Indian saint and scholar. One of his statements adorns my desk:

> Let the dead past bury its dead. The infinite future is before you, there is the inspiring hope that the good thoughts and good deeds are ready with the power of a hundred thousand angels to inspire you always and forever. Arise, awake and stop not till the goal is reached.

From my observations and experiences, I have assembled anecdotes and stories, each of which has taught me some lesson in an intuitive way. I cannot articulate why I learned a particular lesson from some incident but I am able to recognize that the incident had taught me something. Occasionally I would share the incidents and the inchoate lessons with a willing audience.

I also had some opportunities to speak on the subject of leading at the Tata Management Training Centre (TMTC), and earlier in my career at Gulita, the training centre of Hindustan Lever, at business schools and at management forums. I used these occasions to share stories and lessons about personal learning. Over time, I gathered a bunch of speeches and presentations.

In 2003 the All India Management Association initiated an engaging series, called Shaping Young Minds Programme, where business leaders would address young students. I got a first-hand account of other leaders' stories through this series. I also got to see how eager, young minds lapped up the narratives and the lessons. Young people seemed to value the learning embedded in others' leadership narratives and learning.

In 2006 I wrote a column called 'Career Track' for several weeks in the *Economic Times*. This was well received and it also helped me accumulate further material.

In 2008 I remarked to a management school faculty that their institute should learn to teach what cannot be taught. In hindsight, even to me, this statement sounded intriguing. How would an institute achieve this vague objective, even though it was tantalizingly desirable? I was influenced by the perspective advanced by Noel Tichy that experienced operating managers must develop a teachable point of view.[2]

A faculty member at the Indian Institute of Management Ahmedabad (IIMA), Professor Atanu Ghosh, offered to collaborate with me in launching a specially designed programme. In early 2009 I piloted a programme called Learning What's Not Taught (LWNT) as an elective at IIMA, and the students found it immensely helpful.

Since then, with the help of TMTC, I have fine-tuned the design and pedagogy. I have used the revised material to teach a Tata programme by the same name at the TMTC.

This lengthy explanation is meant to tell you how over a long period of time, like a flower collector, I have picked flowers almost randomly. In hindsight it was not as random as it appeared to me then. Some unconscious mental process was guiding me. I wondered what I was to do with these flowers. How could I arrange them into a coherent garland which would be of some use?

My association with the management research work at TMTC offered me the opportunity. I got tangentially involved with the collaborative research undertaken by TMTC with the Center for Creative Leadership (CCL), North Carolina, on how leaders learn in the Indian context. I found a framework—the framework of three worlds—around which I could arrange my experiences and learning.

The book is arranged in four sections. The first section describes the career of one person and explains the framework through his career. The next three sections delve into the three worlds of the manager—the inner world, the world of relationships and the world of getting things done.

There are several books written by consultants and academics on each aspect of the chapters. Their thesis is bolstered by their years' of research or by an impressive statistical analysis. They also offer rules, tips and exercises on 'how to do it better'.

My book is different because it has been written by a practitioner. I have gleaned my thoughts and lessons at the good old university of hard knocks. So it would, I hope, have a practical basis to whatever it says. A critic could argue that my book does not contain a quick-fix toolkit. It covers a wide area of human behaviour in an anecdotal way and contains 'several books within one book'. I plead guilty.

My objective was to write a book that will make the reader recognize himself in the stories. If he reflects on the matter and adapts the lens through which he sees the world, he will learn. Otherwise he will not learn anything. And it is to the goal of provoking reflection that I have aimed this book.

The lessons that the reader will derive will be uniquely his own, shaped as his mind is by the lens of his own experiences. Since no two people have the same experience lens, each reader will derive a different lesson, one that will be uniquely his own. Above all, the lens must be coated with humility if one has to draw any lesson.

The distinctiveness of this book is that it is completely experiential. Every anecdote is from real life; only the names have been changed. Each anecdote has emanated from my own experience or from the person from whom I have taken the story. I am certain that any manager who reads the book will get the 'aha' feeling periodically, the feeling that he recognizes that experience.

There is one caveat. In essence, such stories are common and the reader is advised not to connect a person he has known with the anecdote. He has a high chance of being wrong.

Can this book substitute experience? Can it make 'manager prodigies' who behave at thirty-five with the maturity of a fifty-year-old? Certainly not. That is not the intent or the likely outcome.

At best, it can advance by a few years the rate of learning of the practising manager. With that limited goal, I offer this book to the reader. I hope it is an easy read, it will play on the mind, it will touch a chord somewhere and it will assist the reader to learn his own lessons without teaching anything by itself.

Acknowledgements

The contents of this book have been assembled over many years. I wish to thank the many colleagues and managers with whom I have been privileged to be associated over these last forty years. Whether or not they intended to teach, I have learned a lot from my interactions with several of them. There would have been no book were it not for these interactions and lessons.

In particular, I am grateful to my old school teacher Father Antoine who introduced me to the Indian sense of 'swikriti'. It is a Sanskrit word which means accepting the validity of many different views without being judgemental and yet following your own way of thinking without offence to anyone.

I thank my family for their patience with my erratic hours and Sudha for her painstaking and dedicated editorial suggestions.

I thank Tata for the generous permission to use materials belonging to its institutions: Tata Management Training Centre for the permission to use their 'Three Frameworks' model and Tata Group Corporate Affairs for permission to use excerpts from their publications.

Russi Lala, the incessant writer and chronicler of Tata history, provided an invaluable library of material from which I have drawn. Thank you, Russi, for your generosity and may you continue your energetic efforts.

I acknowledge the benefit from the many conversations on leadership development with my colleagues over the years, in particular: Ashok Ganguly, Bipin Shah, Bhau Phansalkar, Jagdish Chopra, Tarun Sheth and Rajashekharan Nair in Lever;

Jamshed Irani, B. Muthuraman, Ishaat Hussain, S. Ramadorai, Kishor Chaukar, Prasad Menon, Satish Pradhan, Paddy Padmanabhan and Homi Khusrokhan in Tata.

I wish to thank my parents, who, like all parents, imparted to me my early lessons on the subject of complex human relationship—through mythology and stories. One story that I recall merits a mention.

'Avvai' in Tamil literally means a benign, old lady or a grandmother. During the ninth century, there lived a wise, Tamil poet called Avvaiyar. She spread noble thoughts by narrating stories at various courts and kingdoms.

One day she sat under a fruit tree. A little boy, perched on the tree, called out to ask if she would like some fruit. She said 'yes' and the boy asked whether she wanted roasted or unroasted fruits. An astonished and somewhat dismissive Avvaiyar asked for unroasted. How ridiculous to think that fruits could be roasted, anyway?

When the boy shook the tree and fruits fell to the ground, Avvaiyar blew on the fruit to get the dust out before biting into the fruit. The boy expressed wonder that a wise person like her wished to blow on 'an unroasted fruit', which possessed no heat to be blown away.

Avvaiyar realized the message: what the boy had meant in his question and what she understood of his question were quite different. To understand a question or suggestion properly, you must be humble.

She came up with the famous line, 'What we know is but a fistful; what we do not know is the entire universe.' Everyone 'knows' this, but few are 'aware' of this. Awareness increases the desire to know.

I dedicate this book to that human craving of becoming humble by being aware.

PART I

A FRAMEWORK

CHAPTER 1

The Unique Career of Ram

'You cannot teach a man anything; you can only help him find it within himself.'—Galileo

Ram's career was a roller-coaster ride. This story is about his career. A vicarious peek into another's career story affords a lot of practical learning.

Ram was born in 1912. At sixty, he retired as the chief purchasing manager of a multinational company. He felt that he had enjoyed a satisfying career though there were many ups and downs. Every Sunday, one of his sons would visit the retired patriarch and they would talk about the family.

One Sunday in 1989 Ram's eldest son visited him. Ram was lying down, relaxed and cheerful, but looked a little tired. Ram requested his son to pass him some medicine. Before the medicine could be handed over, Ram was gone.

The son was taken aback by the suddenness of the incident and shocked by the actual occurrence of the inevitable. Ram died on Sunday, 18 June 1989 at the age of seventy-seven.

Ram left behind his wife and eighteen immediate family members, his children and his grandchildren. Every member of the clan managed to arrive in the city in time for the cremation.

Ram moved on from this world with the fondest of farewells from each person in his large, happy family; he died in a trice without suffering or pain. Friends and relatives observed that Ram had died a contented man after a unique career.

But what was so unique or special about Ram's career? It was the story of every common person, the story of a small-town boy who made a career in the city. He was not a well-known hotshot who had been decorated by the government or had streets named after him. Surely those are criteria that should determine whether a career is unique!

On the other hand, just as every human being is unique and special, isn't every career unique and special? Each experience teaches a person distinct lessons. Those lessons stay with him and remain uniquely his. To that extent every career is unique.

If one could see Ram's career journey through the lens of his experience and how those experiences influenced and shaped him, his career would appear unique—there were so many quirky twists and turns, so many surprises, so many ambitions, hopes and disappointments. There were many unplanned and extraordinary events; there were great times and awful moments, highs and lows, wins and losses.

So here is the story of Ram's career, which occupied more than half of his physical time and perhaps three quarters of his psychological time during the seventy-seven years of his life.

Overcoming Obstacles

Ram was born in a remote southern village into a family of modest means; life in the village was the way life was in most Indian villages at the start of the twentieth century—no electricity, no running water, a five-kilometre walk to school, a rich tradition of mythology, a vibrant culture of storytelling and a warm, caring extended family.

When he was young, Ram was afflicted with polio. Medical facilities were limited in the village but the elders had some home remedies. The women of the village recommended herbal oils, which were massaged into the boy's affected leg, his right leg. In due course, he would need to exercise his leg by walking long distances. It could provide some relief. If it did not, then it would be his fate and God's will!

With this being the only available treatment and with the family thinking positively, everybody felt that the child had a good chance of being normal. And, sure enough, that is what happened. By the time Ram was twelve, he had overcome his limp. He was able to resume his schooling, which had been interrupted.

By today's urban standards, his schooling was physically very strenuous. He had to walk a long distance to get to school. Ram undertook the walk diligently, because there was no alternative and also because it would help him get rid of the traces of a limp (*see* Box 1.1).

Ram harboured an intense desire to overcome polio. So he did whatever it took to eliminate its damaging effects. This fighting quality stayed with him throughout and perhaps that is what made him a person who wished to overcome any obstacle that arose. During his adult years, Ram was an advocate and promoter of Norman Vincent Peale's *The Power of Positive Thinking*, the seeds of which had perhaps been embedded in his childlike mind. He could not take things as they came and he became intensely motivated to change the deck of cards that life dealt him.

Box 1.1   First Lessons

Teaching aids in schools were rudimentary. Learning orally came naturally to village kids. After all, four thousand years earlier, had not the entire Vedas been passed from generation to generation orally?

Ram's first lessons in writing were not with a pencil on paper, but with a sharp stick or the forefinger on a soft mud surface. Soon he graduated to owning a slate and a slate-stick. There was no abacus in the village; seashells were used to learn arithmetic. Tables were learnt by rote. Once arithmetic was embedded strongly in the mind at such a young age, it conferred an amazing facility with numbers right through life.

Years later, when Ram worked for a foreign company in Calcutta, he would demonstrate his prowess in maths with great aplomb, muttering the numbers in his rapid-fire Tamil. He recalled with great glee, 'I could add and multiply so quickly, but my English bosses would struggle!' He used to relate such anecdotes with the zest of a person who wished to demonstrate how smart he was compared to the foreigners when, in reality, there was no provocation to prove the point.

Seizing Opportunities

However, overcoming obstacles is only one part of a career; the other is seizing opportunities.

Ram found that his career had been decided for him by his well-intentioned and anxious father. Since Ram was afflicted with a weak leg, his father decided that he would be the son to stay in the village and tend the family's small paddy farm. The more able-bodied brothers and cousins could venture out into the big city to seek a career.

Ram found this unfair. He had to do something to change the decision of his well-intentioned father.

Ram was gregarious, voluble and an extrovert, and these characteristics stayed with him through his life—often to his advantage, but sometimes to his disadvantage. In the small and close-knit village community, a talkative person was easily noticed.

In 1930 a group of elderly village widows was planning a pilgrimage to holy places all over the country. They approached Ram with the proposal that he accompany them on their train travels. Train travel had its own challenges in those days (*see* Box 1.2). The women were impressed by his capabilities as he discussed the plan with them. Perhaps his ready wit and gregarious nature appealed to the group weary of the austere village existence.

He offered to perform all the duties expected of him during the long journey; as for him, he had only two conditions: first, that they pay his third-class fare and expenses; second, that he get off at Calcutta. Would they please handle the last leg of their journey without him? They might not have been very excited by this proposition, but they nodded their assent.

Next, Ram had to persuade his stern father, who seldom demonstrated warmth or affection. He was known to be spartan in his personal habits and unwavering in his decisions. How would he tackle his father? Unless his father was won over, the question of leaving the village would not arise. Ram needed a strategy, which he devised intuitively.

Box 1.2   On Track

Apart from the religious angle, a pilgrimage possibly gave the widows a break from their isolated monotony in the village. They could hardly plan a holiday to a hill resort, but a trip to Badrinath or Varanasi met with wide social approval among the village community.

Rail travel had its own hazards and challenges in those days. It took a couple of months to travel by rail to visit the major pilgrim centres of India. The widows would, of course, carry their own food rations for the entire journey, but the assistance of a young lad was always welcome to perform errands at railway stations.

Ram decided to enlist the help of his uncle, his father's elder brother, who was the head of the family. The uncle listened to his spirited nephew's dreams and ideas and was moved. He blessed him and gifted him what was then a princely sum of Rs 100 with the advice that should he be successful in Calcutta, he should help his less privileged cousins and siblings. He undertook the task of persuading Ram's father to permit him to leave the village and seek his dreams in the big city of Calcutta.

And that is how in 1931 Ram, all of nineteen, found himself in Calcutta during the Dassera festival, under a common roof with his brother and his cousin, ready to face the bustling metropolis.

Breaking Some Rules

Ram decided to become a stenographer, a word that few can understand today. Stenographers were in demand among the mercantile offices in Calcutta. All his acquaintances had enrolled to take lessons, and so did Ram.

The initial years in Calcutta posed many challenges. Apart from learning new skills, he had to adjust to a strange city. He spoke Tamil, but the people in the city spoke unfamiliar languages, Bengali and a bit of Hindi. So English became his language of communication. Even after many years, his Hindi and Bengali were interspersed with generous doses of Tamil. The new city and its work environment brought forth novel challenges, and Ram had to contend with peculiar food and patterns of dress. But he adapted and learned from his experiences every day.

After mastering stenography, he secured an office job for a salary of Rs 40 a month. This enabled him to become a contributor to the family rather than remain a dependent; he recalled later that it boosted his self-esteem and built his self-confidence. It also encouraged him to think independently about what would be good for his career.

Soon he made an iconoclastic resolve. He decided to change his hairstyle from the traditional tonsure and pigtail to the normal city haircut. To a traditional person in those days, this was a revolt, totally against social sanction. To his parents and relatives back in the village, this was an early sign of the 'rapid deterioration' in the standards of their dear son. To others, it was the first sign of the different character of this boy.

For an extrovert, sitting in an office for several hours was boring. After a few years, Ram made his second iconoclastic decision—to quit his job. Those were days when no middle-class lad quit a job. He landed a job in the sales organization of a tobacco company called Carreras, which was a predecessor to today's Imperial Tobacco Company (ITC).

His job was to sell cigarettes in Orissa and Andhra. This act of quitting a safe and steady job for an unknown job was further evidence to the family that the lad had set out on a risky path. A Brahmin boy selling cigarettes—gosh, soon they would even smell strange odours emanating from his breath!

What cigarette selling did to Ram was to build in him supreme self-confidence. He met different kinds of people—distributors, retailers, competitors' salesmen, company managers and many more. As a newcomer, he had to do some jobs himself; but for some jobs, for the first time, he relied on others like the distributor or the clearing agent or his coworkers. He began to learn that getting work done through others is at the heart of a manager's job.

Ram travelled widely and observed customs and beliefs that were quite different from those he had learned at home.

He had to discuss and solve transactional business issues such as orders, payments, logistics and merchandising. While travelling, he also got to observe his bosses at close quarters, all their ingenuity, all their frailties and the fickleness of human nature. Such travel and field selling brought with it the uncertainties and insecurities of field work, but he would not trade them for the more comfortable atmosphere of a staid office in Calcutta.

After a few years, Ram decided it was time to return to Calcutta. With a contemporary hairstyle and the confident gait of a successful and ambitious salesman, Ram came back to do something different, but he was not sure what that different thing would be.

A career evolves in strange and unplanned ways. When you are young, you are prone to believing that you can plan your career. But sometimes influences deflect you into unplanned pathways, the consequence of which you appreciate much later (read the story of Dave in chapter 7).

Ram met an older friend, who advised him to become a GDA. He said that it would offer great opportunities to earn money steadily. What was a GDA, Ram asked. Soon he enrolled for the Government Diploma in Accountancy which was a predecessor of the Indian chartered accountancy qualification. This chance encounter with a friend set Ram on a completely different course. A foreign insurance company announced that it had a vacancy in its accounts department. Ram decided to have a go at it.

His ready wit and grasp of numbers endeared him to the foreign bosses. He began a steep climb up the organization. He became a member of the clubs in Calcutta. Soon, he could hold his drink at a party and enjoy the company of those who attended the mercantile socials that were common in the Calcutta of those days. The very middle class Ram was on his way to becoming part of the upper echelons of Calcutta.

Sense of Compassion and Empathy

Ram developed a great empathy for the less fortunate. He treated them with compassion and alleviated their problems whenever he could. It is possible that his early physical difficulties nurtured this sense of compassion in him. His altruism manifested itself in his response to the terrible Bengal famine of 1943.

The Second World War was on and Indian troops fought alongside the Allies. Yet a strong feeling spread in Bengal that the British administration had mismanaged the distribution of food, as the rest of India did not face a famine. Estimates of deaths in Bengal ranged widely from 4 million to 12 million.

Ram set up a kitchen for the poor in south Calcutta, where he lived. He donated money and collected more from others. More important, he gave of himself by cooking and serving the afflicted and the starving. He derived immense satisfaction from setting up his famine kitchen, a constructive step towards alleviating a grave problem. Years later when Ram died, an observer wrote to the family about Ram's selfless service during the Bengal famine.

He evinced a sense of empathy when he stepped in to help needy relatives. Ram was forever grateful to his uncle for encouraging him to leave the village and also for parting with a huge sum of Rs 100 as a blessing. His uncle had said, 'I pray that you earn many times this amount during your career. Use part of that money to support your relatives, some of whom will be less fortunate than you.' Ram took the advice seriously; he would often recount his uncle's advice and how he unhesitatingly accepted the responsibility of educating some of his nephews and bearing the marriage expenses of some of his nieces. Like his brothers, he too shared the accident of his prosperity with indigent and needy relatives throughout his life.

When India became independent in 1947, Ram got an unplanned and unexpected break. Many foreigners left the country. Top-level vacancies within companies were now available to Indians. Ram was lucky to have joined a foreign insurance company where he had established a good reputation. As a result he was appointed to the senior role of Chief Accountant and Company Secretary, one of the three top posts held by Indians in the company. His salary was Rs 1500 per month, a magnificent salary in the early 1950s. Truly he had arrived!

Success and Bonsai Traps

It is axiomatic that precisely when you attain success, the seeds of your weakness begin to sprout. What was earlier a strong point now manifests itself as a weakness. When a strength becomes a weakness, it traps an individual. I call this a bonsai trap because the person does not know that the strength has become a weakness. These manifest as dilemmas or problems which have to be solved.

The other top posts in the insurance company were held by two fellow Indians. Both were sons of wealthy top professionals in Madras. In fact, both had been to England for higher studies, were eminently qualified and had the right background in the perception of the European bosses. While in his own perception, Ram felt equal to the other two, he was unhappy that he was not regarded so by others.

It was not clear whether there really was a problem or whether Ram had worked himself into believing that there was a problem. By the mid 1950s, he had worked himself into a frenzy. He had convinced himself that he was not being accorded his due by his employer be it salary, respect or status. What bothered him was not so much the attitude of the employer as the inferior treatment meted out to him.

The feeling of unhappiness because someone else is treated 'unfairly better' is quite common in management careers. It is surprising how self-destructive the responses of managers can be when they try to remedy their perceived unfair treatment. Every manager has experienced this at some stage of his career.

Ram discussed his predicament with close friends. He talked over the matter with his wife, who had uncanny common sense. His wife advised him to be patient and not to disturb the equilibrium of relationships. She felt that with six kids to be raised, family life was not to be disturbed under any circumstances. His friends gave him similar advice. But Ram continued to be restless.

He felt that as he was only in his mid forties, he should seek out a fairer future for himself rather than accept an injustice. At his workplace, his habit of questioning was viewed as intrusive and not playing the team game well enough. His iconoclastic nature and his extroverted, gregarious personality had served him well all these years, but now played to his disadvantage.

Soon after, he resigned from the company, with the supreme confidence that many would be waiting to offer him a top job immediately. He felt righteous about the act of resigning, almost triumphant. But subsequent developments posed many difficulties for him.

No acceptable full-time job materialized for four years. Potential employers seemed to note that he 'was not even a graduate'. Ram had never imagined that this would be a disqualification, considering he had over twenty years of work experience. The lack of a college degree had not obstructed his career path in the insurance company, where he had joined at the bottom and worked his way up. Sure there were offers for a job, but with a smaller salary, lower status or at an inconvenient location.

With a large family to support, he dipped into his savings. Not having enjoyed higher education himself, he would not consider diminishing the quality or the extent of expenditure on the education and upbringing of his children. There was nothing to economize on except for minor domestic expenses, a few parties or movies.

The very attribute that had made him a leader for almost twenty years, self-esteem, now took a beating, bruising his ego and pricking his pride. The fighter in him stood him in good stead as he suffered through four years of uncertainty.

Painfully but consistently, Ram's effervescence was eroded as he approached the age of fifty.

The Penny Drops: Learning What's Not Taught

Difficulties, hardships and dilemmas teach us the most in our lives. We learn from those experiences, but we learn only by unconsciously developing a personal learning agenda. When such learning occurs, we sense that the penny has dropped, and we get the 'aha' feeling.

For Ram, at this stage, the penny dropped. It was a terrifying but liberating moment. He realized that he had better stop trying to recreate his past. He had to start afresh. He grabbed a job in faraway Bombay in a different industry in a different role and at a lower salary. He decided to make up for lost time in the final ten years of his career.

Luckily for Ram, his new role was in a pharmaceutical sales organization; all the field lessons he had learned earlier in his career came tumbling out of the deep recesses of his mind. Gradually he made his mark again. His personality was sobered by the adversities that he had had to encounter. His work was appreciated in the new company and he rapidly gained recognition. But one ambition that he had secretly harboured for years, to be appointed member of a company's leadership team and be designated 'Company Director', was never fulfilled. He retired as the chief purchasing manager, a senior management role, but not quite what he had dreamt of.

Before Ram died, it was a great solace to him that his sons were ultimately appointed company directors. Times had changed and it meant something quite different; nonetheless, he found it hugely satisfying. He could die with a smile on his face.

Unique Defined

Was Ram's career unique? How different was it from that of many executives who build a career in a city?

Evolutionary biologists tell us that 60 per cent of the genes in a banana are the same as those in a human being. The difference between chimpanzees and human beings is extremely small when viewed from the perspective of a geneticist. Chimpanzees have twenty-four pairs of chromosomes; some five million years ago, two chromosomes fused to evolve into a species with twenty-three pairs of chromosomes. That species is the human being.

Apart from this difference, there is not much to set a chimpanzee apart from a human being—humans are 98 per cent chimpanzee. That one chromosome took thousands of years to play out its effect; 6 billion human beings on this planet now have an identical number of chromosome pairs—and yet we hold our species to be distinct from chimps; indeed we hold each human being to be unique.

We need a framework to think about career experiences, the lessons they offer and what makes them unique and special. The narrative illustrates what helps a person to become aware of, and transcend, himself. It is the bedrock of leadership development methodology.

That is why I begin this book with a career story. A peek into someone else's story helps us appreciate the lessons in a practical way.

Box 1.3
KEY MESSAGES

The most important lessons are not taught to you.
You learn them yourself through your experiences.

⸺

Your experiences are unique to you.
They can teach you lessons if you seek the lessons.

⸺

The experience is not important.
What you do with the experience is important.

⸺

Constant adaptation to emerging circumstances
is an essential part of your learning.

⸺

Reading about the learning experiences of others
and listening to their stories accelerates learning.

CHAPTER 2

The Framework of Three Worlds

'Nature does not give a man virtue; the process of becoming a good man is an art.'—Lucius Seneca

Over the years, I have been jotting down interesting incidents and experiences. It is now a source I draw upon during my reflections on leadership, ambition, frailty and success. I spent some time searching for a framework through which I could interpret these experiences so that they became useful lessons for leadership development. This represented my personal learning agenda. This is the way we all learn what's not taught to us.

The process of writing *The Case of the Bonsai Manager*, my first book, on the importance of intuition for managers gave me immense joy.[1] It also raised new thoughts and dilemmas in my mind.

I wondered where the balance lay between acquiring and displaying positive success skills, while simultaneously avoiding the diluting effects of weaknesses and negative traits that every human being has. I refer to these negative traits as 'bonsai traps'.

Management practice and leadership development are focused on developing the positive: successful leaders learn positive techniques and skills, which can give them a competitive advantage. When two people at the same level compete for a promotion, their understanding and application of these positive skills will come into play and this will decide their future. How important is it to become aware of the negatives that each leader has hard-wired into him? Who will point them out and train the manager to suppress their effects? Do leaders ponder about the need to suppress these negative attributes? Perhaps not too much. Managers, especially during the early years of their career, tend not to think about their own negative traits.

As the career progresses, at certain stages, the penny drops for each manager with regard to his negatives. Such incidents offer great personal lessons and they are unique to that person. The circumstances of such incidents create emotions in the individual and, when he reflects upon these emotions, he learns. This is true of every good manager and leader. This is how experiences translate into learning and learning to wisdom.

A framework is needed to reflect upon such matters.

TMTC-CCL Framework

The Tata Management Training Centre (TMTC) in Pune has a small team of academics who engage in practical and usable research on matters that are of strategic value to the group's companies. In 2006 TMTC undertook a research project on leadership in cooperation with the Center for Creative Leadership (CCL) in North Carolina.

Among the first pieces of work done jointly was data collection and analysis from Indian business executives to sharpen the findings of CCL (*see* Box 2.1).[2] The India research study set out to discover the answers to the CCL's two questions on leadership development:

- *What* kind of lessons do leaders in India usually learn?
- *How* do they learn these lessons?

Nearly seventy-one successful Indian managers were interviewed for the study—a decent number, considering that the original CCL work was done by interviewing 191 American managers. The objective was to factor in the cultural and contextual differences into an Indian adaptation of the original study.

While there was a broad resemblance between international data and Indian data, there were differences in the points of emphasis and the hierarchy of influences. For example, in the

Box 2.1   Centre for Creative Leadership

Over the years, CCL has developed a robust and successful leadership practice at their centre. The trailblazing LoE (Lessons of Experience) study was conducted in the United States in the 1980s in a quest to find answers to the many queries on leadership development. Its core lay in the data from four separate studies encompassing 191 successful executives from six major corporations. These 191 executives had responded to two questions on events that led to a lasting change in them as managers:

- What happened?
- How did you learn?

As the leadership development guru Warren Bennis observed in his foreword, 'The principal merit of The Lessons of Experience is its gut truth: the primary responsibility for effective management development resides in the managers themselves.'[3]

The broad findings of such mega studies are universally applicable in a general way; local-level tweaking is relevant and helpful to provide a better instrument for application in that country. It was this context that led Tata to collaborate with CCL.

Indian study data, there was greater emphasis on giving young people early responsibility and on allowing them to find their own way out of the difficulties arising from assignments. Greater importance was given to the learning of soft skills. This probably emanated from the more traditional family structure and longer parental influence on the Indian manager as compared to his western counterpart.

The interviewees had to identify at least three significant or memorable events in their life, events that led to a lasting transformation in their approach to management. Each of the events listed was probed by the researchers to identify what had been learned and how that learning had occurred.

The findings on what lessons were learned were classified into certain broad types. They pertained to what the researchers called the three worlds (*see* Box 2.2).

The first one is an inner world. It is about lessons relating to the person, including strengths and weaknesses.

The second and third worlds are the external worlds: the world of getting things done and the world of relationships with others.

The leadership lessons are equally distributed among these three worlds, suggesting that a company's leadership development actions must be equally balanced to include all the three worlds.

The story of Ram touched upon all three worlds.

The Inner World

In the inner world, there are nine lessons, which are described below.

The most important lesson in the inner world is developing self-confidence. Self-confidence is outward-directed and is quite different from arrogance, which is inward-directed. For Ram, the polio affliction in his childhood was potentially detrimental to his self-confidence. Ram was determined to overcome this. The affliction, far from leading to depression, gave rise to a fighting spirit. This was bolstered when he figured out how to escape from the village to the big city. While everybody experiences such incidents, not everyone emerges from the experience with renewed self-confidence.

The second lesson is self-awareness. It is natural to become aware of your strengths. It is harder to become aware of your weaknesses. In Ram's case, he was always keen on doing something different to seek ways of advancement; he seemed to have developed an early awareness that his outgoing nature would be a distinctive competence. This is illustrated by his persuading his father to permit him to accompany the widows on their pilgrimage. Ram worked on this to his full advantage. In fact, it is possible that he may have momentarily erred when he miscalculated his strengths and resigned from his job in Calcutta. He had underestimated what it would take a manager like him in the 1950s to land another job.

The third important lesson in the inner world is about life goals. In India children tend to stay with their families into adulthood and their relationship with the family is lifelong. Setting independent life goals is sometimes perceived as being self-centred. Ram's willingness to quit his job and opt for a more contemporary hairstyle was motivated by his sense of what he wished to achieve. He seemed to want one thing very badly, to be a company director. He did not allow his ambition to consume him, but achieved this vicariously through his sons.

The next lessons pertain to becoming humane, building credibility and dealing with ambiguity.

Ram had a good sense of empathy for others as demonstrated by his desire to help those less fortunate. During the Bengal famine, he set up a kitchen to help the larger community. By assisting his relatives, he fulfilled the commitment he had made to his uncle when he left the village. It became extremely important for him to be as generous as possible within his family circle.

Ram built a bank of professional credibility through his work in the insurance company. When he quit in a huff, he found that his bank balance as well as his credibility was being eroded. He learned from his mistake; he painstakingly rebuilt both his career and his credibility in a new city, in a new industry and in a new company, all the time subdued by the humbling experience he had undergone.

In dealing with ambiguity, Ram probably learned big lessons. He had to coexist in comfort in both the traditional society and the modern, urban society. On the one hand, he could be perfectly comfortable wearing a black tie and dinner jacket to a Calcutta cocktail party discussing industrial policies or politics in India and, on the other, he could be equally at ease wearing a traditional dhoti and caste mark to a religious function and conversing about spirituality. Many Indians are able to live in multiple worlds simultaneously and comfortably.

The last three lessons are about coping with setbacks, developing adaptability and maintaining integrity. Ram seemed to get into troubled waters from time to time, first, when he quit a steady job as a stenographer, then by veering off course to study accountancy and finally by leaving a high-paying corporate job at the peak of his career. But he invariably figured a way out.

He had to develop adaptability, but by learning his own lessons. For example, it took him all the four years of virtual joblessness to become practical about what kind of job and salary he would accept. As the saying goes, adversity is the best teacher and, for sure, Ram learned from his adversities.

Box 2.2	Lessons Learned in the Three Worlds	
Inner World (35%)	World of Getting Things Done (32%)	World of People (33%)
Confidence	Being execution- and operation-savvy	Managing and motivating subordinates
Self-awareness	Improving management and leadership skills	Nurturing and developing subordinates
Life goals	Grasping the technical aspects of running a business	Team management
Becoming humane	Acquiring a broad organizational view and strategic insight	Building relationships with peers and superiors
Building credibility	Becoming adept at decision making and problem solving	Communication and feedback
Dealing with ambiguity	Handling organizational change	Customer orientation
Coping with setbacks		
Developing flexibility and adaptability		
Integrity		

Source: Lessons Leaders Learn, TMTC Pune, 2008

The last point about maintaining integrity is not about financial integrity. It is about being true to yourself. Doubts are bound to arise as a part of life, but it is your sense of integrity that allows you to live your life fully. For example, Ram's deep sense of being middle class and religious helped him avoid the pitfalls of the city and commerce, though his adoption of the city hairstyle and socializing habits made his well-wishers wonder whether his ethical standards too would decline in due course.

The World of Getting Things Done

The research mentions six lessons from the world of getting things done:

The most important lesson is to become action-oriented and get things done. Academics are often seen to be lacking in this respect, but for an industrial manager it is his life blood. Recall how Ram wanted to do things rather than watch things happen. He seemed to exemplify the now widely accepted view that a manager's development happens for the 99 per cent of the time when he is doing things and at best 1 per cent in classrooms.

The second lesson is the improvement of leadership skills. This refers to the ability to get others to do what is decided. The leader must be able to depart from his zone of comfort to lead such an effort. Ram did not seem to value the comfort of doing the same thing; he would not let the grass grow under his feet, so he went out of his way to try new tasks and learn from them.

The third important lesson is to get a firm grasp of the technicalities of the job. This is the way to build credibility with the people who will work for you. Ram seemed to learn the technical skills of his job instinctively and then sought to acquire the skills of the next level. First, he learned stenography. Then he went out and managed customers in the field. Then he came back to learn accounting. Then he went on to learn how to get things done by other people.

The other three lessons in the world of getting things done relate to developing a broader view of the tasks at hand, becoming skilled at decision making and handling change. Ram's career shows how he gradually learned to be a management 'architect' rather than just an 'engineer'. Early in life, he grasped that you have to decide and solve problems; you cannot keep analysing and thinking except for a short while. He learned how to adjust to different bosses in different companies; he learned the art of persuasion and communication, both of which are essential drivers of organizational change.

The world of getting things done is vital to a management leader's role. Managers are required to get things done, not to do them—and there is a skill involved (*see* Box 2.3).

Box 2.3   Learning to Be a Manager

Tachi Yamada, MD, is president of the Bill and Melinda Gates Foundation's Global Health Program. Here is what he told Adam Bryant when asked how he first learned to be a manager:

'I think the most difficult transition for anybody from being a worker bee to a manager is this issue of delegation. What do you give up? How can you have the team do what you would do yourself without your actually doing it? . . . I learned a principle that I apply today—I don't micromanage, but I have microinterest. I do know the details and I do care about the details. I feel like I have an intimate knowledge of what is going on, but I don't tell people what to do.'

Source: International Herald Tribune, 1 March 2010

The World of People

Six lessons were mentioned in the research report from the world of people:

Nobody can be a leader if he cannot motivate his subordinates. It is easily the most important lesson. It is not essential to be a gregarious person to motivate others. But it often helps. Being a people-oriented and an outgoing personality, Ram took to managing others quite easily. His former subordinates spoke glowingly about these qualities in later years.

The second lesson from this world is the ability to nurture subordinates. While Ram's story outlined in chapter one does not throw any direct light on this aspect, Ram took great pride in being associated with the early successes of some top managers.

Managing teams is the third lesson. Ram's sales stints showed up this skill particularly well. Later in his career, he faced a tough labour union problem in his region. Through empathy and vigour, he was reported to have held the management team's morale at a high level despite innumerable threats.

The other three lessons pertain to relationships with peers and subordinates, customers, and communication. The narration of Ram's story does not throw much light on these aspects, but they will be the subject of some comments later in the book.

The essential point is that you learn your lessons from reflecting on your own experiences.

Where Ram Learned His Lessons

Learning from such reflections and ruminations can be confounding. Very often they lead to confusion and bewilderment. You may even wonder whether the career you have enjoyed has been meaningful or personally rewarding. Such thoughts even passed through the mind of Yudhishtira in the epic *Mahabharata* (*see* Box 2.4). Reflections about a career often lead to such thoughts. Modern organizational psychologists call it 'mid-life crisis'. Surely, it is more than that!

Interestingly Ram never attended any advanced management course. It is safe to assume that he may have attended some minimalist courses during his long career. However, the influence of formal training in leadership development does not seem to

---

Box 2.4   Reflecting on Experiences

The *Mahabharata* is the gripping story of an epic battle between two sets of cousins. It is full of intrigue, envy, lust and suspense. The Pandavas, led by Yudhishtira, eventually won the battle over their Kaurava cousins.

The central piece of the epic is the devastating battle. It was long, complex and took many lives. After winning the bloody fratricidal war, Yudhishtira reflects, 'I have conquered the whole earth . . . but after finishing this killing of my own relations and near ones, a huge remorse fills me . . . did I do the right thing by fighting the war? . . . have I won or, in reality, have I lost?'

---

have been particularly strong. He learned on the job, making mistakes while doing things and remembering to do better the next time.

As the original CCL study reported, learning about learning makes it possible to take control of your education, to learn faster and better, and to adapt across time and circumstances. Your experiences are 'crucibles' that lead you to a new sense of identity. Research shows that 'learning from crucibles occurs when you can connect your personal aspirations, your motivations and your learning style'.[4]

This is an important message. I am often asked by aspiring executives how much of a disadvantage it would have been if they had studied in a less well-known educational institution or had work experience in an unknown company. I always emphasize that what matters is what they can do in the future with their education and experience; this depends on the quality of the education received or work experience acquired. The reputation of the institute or company is a crude and inaccurate surrogate for these measures.

Only 3 per cent of leadership development occurs due to classroom training and coursework, unexpectedly low considering how much managers clamour to attend top-level courses at management institutes these days.

This framework, like many such models, does not provide unexpectedly dramatic findings. It merely offers insights that may help fine-tune how leaders can be developed more successfully.

While the research by TMTC and CCL was about how leaders learn and how their development can be positively triggered, the theme of my book is about overcoming the barriers to leadership development. My quest was for a framework to help potential leaders become aware of the bonsai traps during their career.

The framework could well be the same. Triggers and barriers are two sides of the same leadership development model.

It is true that Ram's story is the story of every common manager. In each individual, there is as much evidence of boosters, such as ambition, self-confidence, hard work and sheer grit, as bonsai traps, such as arrogance, eccentricity, volatility and jealousy. Every person exhibits in his behaviour a combination of these boosters and bonsai traps.

Each one of us has an extraordinary passage through life and career with exhilarating highs and depressing lows. Any career would have its share of rewarding and frustrating experiences, the career may be well known or unknown in the public domain and it may qualitatively be a rich one or a poor one. But every career story offers invaluable lessons to an observer who cares to reflect about the story.

Box 2.5
KEY MESSAGES

You need to learn certain lessons which
nobody teaches you.

You learn unique lessons by reflecting upon
your own experiences.

Two people who go through the same experience
learn different lessons.

You learn by integrating your personal aspirations,
your motivations and your learning style.

You learn through experiences in your inner
world, the world of relationships and the
world of doing things.

CHAPTER 3

Explicit Feedback
The Clementine Mirror

'Ignorance more frequently begets confidence than knowledge. Most of what I learnt is self-taught.'—Charles Darwin

Every leader's grand ambitions are embedded within that person's mental make-up. His unique background and the testing times he has been through are the basis on which his ambition stands. To any person, his dreams and ambition are self-evident and unique, though they may not appear so to others.

The development of leadership in a person is an evolutionary and complex process. There is much more to it than acquiring and mastering explicit knowledge. The model of three worlds indicates that leaders learn and develop in their inner world, the world of people and the world of getting things done. Managers learn lessons through their insights and experiences. By definition, insight is experiential and cannot be taught or preached. At best, metaphors and allegories may help.

While the triggers for the development of a top leader arise from these three worlds, the barriers which prevent a leader from achieving his full potential also emanate from these three worlds! Triggers and barriers are like the yin and the yang of Tao.

A Bonsai Trap: 'I Am Better Than Others'

For the past several years, I have been conducting an informal exercise whenever I meet managers in classrooms within the Tata group and elsewhere. I write down two statements for each person to answer either in the positive or in the negative.

First, 'I am more competent at work than those whom I consider my peers.' Second, 'I have better human relations compared to those whom I consider my peers.'

Statistical logic would suggest that the aggregate of all the answers received over a period of time should be around 50 per cent, assuming that the competent managers who attend compare themselves with competent peers. I got a number close to 80 per cent, which means that most people thought they were better than others. This is the 'I am better than others' trap into which every person is prone to fall.

According to common sense, managers and indeed all human beings tend to hold overly favourable views of their abilities. For the doubters, there is evidence to back this view.[1] This apparently simple research finding points to two dangers that confront every manager.

First is the obvious danger that you are prone to exaggerate your strengths and play down your weaknesses when you compare yourself with others. Second is the danger that, by not being aware of this tendency, you are prone to miss whatever feedback and signals come to you.

It is a common trap for us to overestimate our strengths and to underestimate our weaknesses. This is the root cause of indignation on being passed over for a promotion and it also triggers the resentful perception of getting less favour and attention from the boss when compared to a colleague. It is a universal bonsai trap. Associated with this basic trap are a number of other traps: arrogance, insensitivity and envy, among others.

It is difficult for a manager to shake off his bonsai traps or dark spots. At best, he can become aware of their existence and learn to manage them.

A deep sense of self-realization is required to appreciate your weaknesses. You learn about your behavioural bonsai traps all by yourself. Nobody tells you about them.

It is often said that if you really care about somebody, you give them constructive feedback. If you do not care about somebody, you say only positive things. However, in reality, that is not the way the world works.

Very little is told to you by your boss or colleagues about the negative manifestations of your bonsai traps. Why should your peer do so when it is none of his business? And why should your senior do so lest he be regarded as a nagging senior? Why should your subordinate risk his career by doing so? Some bonsai traps do only minor damage, while some others do heavy damage. The positives and negatives progressively accumulate, and when taken together define who you are perceived to be.

And then, one day, the penny drops for you.

To be aware of your bonsai traps, you must learn to listen and sense the effect you are having on others. People are constantly giving you feedback without intending to do so. Some are explicit, while most are implicit. In this chapter, examples of explicit feedback are discussed.

Explicit Feedback

You can become aware of your dark spots by someone holding a mirror to your behaviour and by looking deep into the mirror. I call the feedback received in this explicit manner the Clementine

Box 3.1   Clementine's Advice

Clementine Churchill had a fierce loyalty to her famous husband, but she rebuked his excesses and tried to repair the fractured chain of his relationships. The country, as much as he, owed a debt to such a wife because she preserved Sir Winston from succumbing to the corruption of wielding absolute authority over the nation.

In June 1940, she wrote him a letter, held it for four days, tore up the letter, finally reconstructed the torn letter, and then sent it. It lies in the archives in that condition and reading the letter tells us why she must have hesitated: remember there was a war going on and Sir Winston was the prime minister.

The letter read as follows:

> My darling, I hope you will forgive me if I tell you something that I feel you ought to know. One of the men in your entourage, a devoted friend, has been to me and told me that there is a danger of your being disliked by your colleagues and subordinates because of your rough, sarcastic and overbearing manner ... If an idea is suggested, say at a conference, you are supposed to be so contemptuous that presently no idea, good or bad, will be forthcoming. I was astonished and upset because in all these years, I have been accustomed to all those who have worked with and under you, loving you—I said this and I was told 'No doubt it is the strain.'

> My darling Winston, I must confess that I have noticed deterioration in your manner; you are not as kind as you used to be ... It is for you to give orders, but with urbanity, kindness, and, if possible, with Olympic calm ... I cannot bear that those who serve the country and yourself should not love you as well as admire and respect you ... Besides you won't get the best results by irascibility and rudeness ... Please forgive your loving, devoted and watchful Clemmie.

mirror, named after the charming letter Clementine Churchill wrote to her husband, Sir Winston (*see* Box 3.1).

Wives are known to render a unique service to their husbands by telling them what no one else dares to. The explicit feedback that a leader can get from the spouse can be harsh, but very valuable.

There are also several techniques of 360 degree feedback available to modern managers. These techniques offer a way to get feedback from colleagues. These can be quite threatening to a manager. I recall an episode at Tata.

A group of senior directors and managers was meeting to discuss the human resources agenda of the group. The subject was self-development, leadership styles and sensitivity.

The HR team had developed a tool by incorporating their learnings while implementing published research. Branded as the Tata Reflections, the subject provoked an animated discussion. Some felt it would serve as a 360 degree feedback, while others wondered whether it would work successfully in the hierarchical Indian social context.

A senior leader, who had had first-hand experience, explained to the group his own experience and the 'aha' moment with the Tata Reflections. He delivered his narration with appropriate sombreness and gravitas:

When I received feedback about how my colleagues and subordinates perceived my behaviour, I felt shattered. I thought I was being decisive, they saw me as plugging a predetermined view; I felt I had allowed everyone to speak, but they thought my body language was discouraging for those who wished to speak up. I thought I differed politely, but they thought I came through as a touch intolerant.

In short, on several counts, what I thought of as my strength appeared to them as a weakness.

I was confounded, so when I got home, I narrated the whole episode to my wife. She said to me, 'You need not have done this expensive exercise. I have been hinting at all these aspects to you and I could have pointed out all this for less money. You should listen to me more carefully!'

Each of us in the room knew that it is the well-meaning spouse who could point out her spouse's dark spots and criticize constructively to produce an effect that no other person can. Seizing the benefit of the Clementine mirror is up to you—it can be taken seriously and worked upon or can rapidly lead to a divorce!

An Unusual Court Judgement

Spouses need not be the only source of explicit feedback. Recently the subject of arrogance on the part of powerful people became the subject of a court judgement.[2]

Angad Das was a humble constable in the Central Reserve Police Force (CRPF). His employer found after several years that Das had submitted a false date of birth certificate at the time of joining. The officer-in-charge was planning a suitable punishment for this offence of falsification.

Before any departmental action was implemented, Das thought he might appeal for compassion. He wrote a very polite letter of appeal to the Additional District Inspector General requesting that he be allowed to continue in service as he had heavy family responsibilities. The court quoted extracts of Das's letter, 'With folded hands and touching your feet, I pray that I may be allowed to complete the service. I may be awarded any other punishment. Seven people depend on my salary and they will all be uprooted, they will resort to beggary and fall on the wrong path to earn their bread.'

The departmental officers were offended by the letter and promptly dismissed him from service, perhaps giving the impression that the cause of dismissal was his letter of appeal. According to the Supreme Court judges, this letter of appeal to review the decision on compassionate grounds received an unwarranted and arrogant reaction from the administration. Such behaviour was unacceptable.

The court 'failed to comprehend how the letter seeking re-employment on compassionate grounds can ever receive such unwarranted and arrogant reaction. The order is wholly arbitrary and illegal . . . People in power and authority should not easily lose their equanimity, composure and appreciation for the problems of lesser mortals . . . Arrogance and vanity have no place in the discharge of official functions and duties . . .'

The court ordered that Das be paid Rs 50,000 for being treated with disdain and be given full pension benefits.

This is as explicit a feedback as you can ever receive for a mistake.

Learning through Mistakes

It is not possible to avoid making mistakes. One can only try to reduce the number and the frequency of their occurrence. Making mistakes in human relations is a characteristic of all leaders. Those around notice these mistakes but do not give feedback.

It is possible to climb out of a trap when one has inadvertently fallen into it. However, you should first try to avoid falling into these traps. A manager must know and admit that he is in a bonsai trap; otherwise there is no chance of his getting out of it. If a bonsai trap becomes a permanent one, leadership capabilities get severely diminished.

Other people's experiences are incredibly valuable. You can see other people's faults easily, and find it very tough to see your own faults. That is why through anecdotes from other people's careers and experiences, you can recognize situations and relate to them with your own.

Personal learning can be accelerated by observing and studying others' experiences. When we carry on our person something repulsive, the repulsiveness of what we carry within ourselves is invisible to us.

Learning requires a high level of self-awareness, understanding other people and getting the best out of relationships and networks. Such expertise is essential for a person to develop and exercise the capability of organizing people around a common goal: inspiring them to work together and achieve certain targeted results by identifying and using opportunities rather than by watching opportunities pass by.

The story that follows was an eye-opener for me.

A Suppressed Hurt

One evening some years ago, a former colleague came home with his son and daughter-in-law. The father wanted to seek our good wishes for the youngsters. Both the bright youngsters had secured admission to an advanced professional college in Boston and BR's family was justifiably proud of their accomplishments.

During our long association, I had been his boss more than once and we had even been neighbours for a few years. So the relationship was not just professional, there was a family connection as well. We had, from time to time, tracked and observed our children grow up and come into their own. It was the kind of relationship that a professional manager experiences after decades of work in a single company.

After the greetings and the customary serving of refreshments, the conversation turned to evocative stories of yesteryears— little incidents that each of us remembered about work, promotions and colleagues.

Suddenly BR, with a twinkle in his eye, recalled one episode, which left me devastated. 'Boss, do you remember that afternoon twenty years ago when you called me and my juniors to your room and lampooned me for the errors in my proposal? Boy, how you reprimanded me in the presence of my colleagues! I felt really small. But I learned some good lessons from the incident. I remember it so well.'

My wife had for long been a quiet, silent reflector or mirror of my behaviour. She had not always been successful in getting me to acknowledge the bonsai traps; however, she had often made me pause and reflect on whether I could have communicated to a colleague or a relation more constructively. And here was one such occasion!

I was shattered for a number of reasons.

First, I had absolutely no recollection of the episode. How could I be completely unaware of an episode which had caused so much hurt to BR? My first reaction was that BR was exaggerating. But I was conscious that my bosses often did not remember the times they had lambasted me. On one particular occasion, many years after the event, I reminded my former chairman of a rough episode. He could not recall anything. He even seemed to deny what I believed to be the facts of the incident. Now the situation was reversed and I could not remember!

Second, BR had never mentioned the incident to me as a grievance or even as an anecdote. But why would he, as long as I was a boss or a senior? Now both of us had moved on.

Third, he was narrating the details of the episode in the presence of his family and mine. For him, there was no embarrassment; it was a natural part of growing in a career. I was the one feeling bad as I had been cast in the role of the tormentor.

Fourth and last, he was recalling the episode with no rancour; rather, there was a trace of mirth in his pleasant voice.

I was uncomfortable, but he was not.

My wife had sometimes pointed out my occasional tendency to talk tough with people without meaning to do so. On this occasion, she said absolutely nothing, but I imagined that my wife gave me that look of 'How many times have I advised you to be careful!'

After BR and his family departed with our warm blessings, I reflected on the episode. It was not as if I had ignored my wife's periodic blandishments though I did resent them occasionally. I knew that she was right about the benefits of avoiding harsh or toxic behaviour.

But paradoxically, I found that it was necessary sometimes to be direct or harsh, to emphasize a point or to infuse greater urgency into team commitment and action. How does one get the balance? Is there an ideal balance? Some people are extra-sensitive and cannot take even slight criticism or behavioural angularity. Others seem more robust.

A lesson I had learned at training programmes and read in books came back to me: those leaders who fail do so not because they are stupid or technically incompetent, but because of the manner in which they behave under certain situations, particularly under stress. Stereotypes of behavioural dangers and their toxic effects have been described elegantly time and again.

How come leaders know of the danger and still brazenly confront danger? If human beings were known to act rationally, history books would be much thinner and far less interesting. There are just a few, perhaps a dozen, behavioural aberrations that people are condemned to be prone to during their careers: arrogance, self-centredness, volatility, excessive caution, distrust and aloofness. It is essential to be sensitive to the occurrence and effects of such dark spots.[3] It is said that great leaders are those who can step on your toes without damaging the sheen on your shoes.

What might have happened in BR's brain after he got a verbal laceration from his boss?

Insights from Brain Science

The brain experiences the workplace as a social system. That is why a career is very important to all of us. We spend as much as half of our lives in our professional career.

Neuroscience suggests that a person is physiologically affected when he feels a sense of rejection.[4]

The activity and response of the brain are similar in two very different situations. When you are offered food which you like or dislike, your brain responds in the same way as when you have an interpersonal exchange which you like or dislike.

When you are reprimanded or given an assignment that you perceive as unworthy or given a poor raise, it is equivalent to being hit on the head. Contrary to popular perception, the brain equates social needs with survival rather than with well-being. You can feel as desperate when you feel socially ostracized or excluded as when you are hungry or physically threatened.

We now know that a bad interpersonal interaction leaves survival-related marks on the brain. No boss would like to inflict such marks on his subordinate. Hence, successful executives should be far more sensitive to the effect of their behaviour on others.

The Clementine mirror provides a reliable way, an explicit way, for a leader to be aware of and become sensitive to the negative behaviour he might inadvertently display.

There is an implicit way of getting feedback and I call that the Vikramaditya experience. This is the subject of the next chapter.

Box 3.2
KEY MESSAGES

Every person is shaped by his crucible experiences.
These produce positive and negative tendencies.

It is difficult to eliminate negative tendencies. You
can develop a heightened sensitivity to their
presence and thus control their effects.

Feedback about negative tendencies can come
through explicit feedback. Most work acquaintances
would not wish to offer any explicit feedback.

The best feedback is from a well-wisher
like a spouse.

CHAPTER 4

Implicit Feedback
The Vikramaditya Experience

'This life is a great chance ... seek for the highest, aim at the highest and you shall reach the highest.'—Swami Vivekananda

In the last chapter, the expression 'Clementine mirror' was used to describe how a person can receive explicit feedback about the effect he has on his peers and co-workers. The mirror effect could be realized through feedback from a close person, or through the use of a 360 degree instrument, or through the engagement of a professional coach.

In this chapter, let us explore the role of implicit feedback. An implicit feedback or signal is picked up by a person in two ways: by developing empathy and by careful listening.

I use the term Vikramaditya experience to describe the pick-up of implicit signals about the feelings and views of co-workers. Vikramaditya is a character from Indian history and mythology (*see* Box 4.1).

Developing Empathy: The Emotional Crucible

The capacity for empathy is innate in humans and is thought to be evident in other species too.[1] An account of elephants in

47

> **Box 4.1 The Incognito King**
>
> In the Ujjain kingdom of the first century BCE, King Vikramaditya appears as a key character. He was famed for his valour, wisdom and magnanimity. He knew that his people would not directly criticize the ruler or give him explicit feedback about the state of the citizen. Therefore, he resorted to incognito tours of his kingdom to listen to and to observe what the common folks had to say about his administration. It was his method of empathizing with his subjects. According to legend, this is how he learned about some of the shortcomings of his administration, which helped him prevent trouble from breaking out.

Burma comes to mind. A mother elephant with her three-month-old calf was reported trapped in a fast-rising torrent in the Upper Taungdwin River. The calf was screaming with terror and, at one stage, was swept away downstream in the torrent. The mother swam after the baby, encircled the calf with her trunk and pulled the baby upstream.

In Kenya, a black rhino and her baby came to a clearing where salt had been left to attract animals.[2] After licking the salt, the baby rhino got stuck in the deep mud. The mother rhino could not rescue the baby in spite of several attempts.

A group of elephants arrived at the salt lick. Seeing the baby rhino stuck, an adult elephant approached the rhino and ran its trunk over it. The mother rhino was incensed and charged at the elephant. This happened a few times. Ethologists wonder why the elephant risked its own safety to rescue the baby rhino even after the mother charged it. Could it have been empathy?

What is empathy and can it be taught?

According to Carol M. Davis, associate professor at the School of Medicine, University of Miami, 'Empathy is a commonly used, but a poorly understood, concept.' Empathy cannot be taught, but it can be facilitated. It cannot be forced. When empathy occurs, we experience it rather than cause it to happen.

Empathy should not be confused with sympathy. Sympathy occurs when you understand another person's situation or plight without actually feeling for him or her. Empathy occurs when you understand and feel for another person's plight.

In the 1920s an American psychologist coined the technical term 'motor mimicry' for the phenomenon of a person physically imitating the distress of another person. It is as though one person has actually entered the world of feelings of another person. This word came to be known as 'empathy'. When one person's emotions are attuned to another person's, empathy occurs. To be attuned to one person's emotions, the other must be calm and receptive (*see* Box 4.2).

There is a close link between developing empathy and your past experiences. That is why a person born with a silver spoon

---

Box 4.2   Chaplin Discovered

It was Charlie Chaplin's sense of empathy that accidentally brought out his natural talent. This story about Charlie Chaplin illustrates how empathy played a major part in launching his career.

Baby Charlie used to live in London with his mother, Hannah, in the late 1890s. Hannah used to entertain rioters and soldiers in the Aldershot Theatre in London. Little Charlie used to accompany her every day. He recalls that her emotions gripped him and he started to emote his mother's roles as he watched her evening after evening.

When Charlie was five years old, Hannah developed a throat problem and she was heckled off the stage by the audience. Charlie was so moved and enraged that he took the stage and sang 'Jack Jones', a well-known tune at that time. The audience was spellbound and threw coins at him. Charlie Chaplin was thus launched into his historic and entrepreneurial career.

in his mouth may find it difficult to empathize with extreme poverty. This aspect is at the core of the story of Jim Stovall's book *The Ultimate Gift*. A wealthy man leaves part of his estate to his grandson provided the grandson undergoes certain grassroots experiences that would teach him valuable lessons in empathy.

Empathy is often born out of having been in a crucible—an experience in which a person has been through difficulties and anxieties. Empathy is born out of being able to feel emotionally what the other person feels. As soon as this state is accomplished in a genuine way, a new perspective or lesson opens up. It is very difficult to achieve this state.

You have to suspend your sense of logic or your natural tendency to examine whether that feeling was legitimate or not. Most arguments arise out of this inability to suspend the tendency to judge and just share the feeling being expressed, between siblings, spouses, friends and colleagues.

An Empathetic Question While Recruiting a Trainee

All endings are also beginnings. Only, we do not know it at that time. Our lives intersect with others at many points without our being aware of it.

In a delightful book, *The Five People You Meet in Heaven*, Mitch Albom narrates the story of an eighty-three-year-old war veteran who dies under the giant wheel in the amusement park where he works. He reaches heaven where he meets five people whom he recognizes. As the story unfolds, he realizes that each one of them had affected his life without his being aware of it.

This is true of managers also. Views from casual acquaintances who are not formally assigned the role of a well-wisher can be extremely valuable. Their ideas come like gentle drops of rain that fall around you without making their presence felt too strongly or being intrusive.

When I grew up in Calcutta, it was a premier mercantile city, still maintaining the famous boxwallah tradition. Any young person walking around the office areas like Fairlie Place and Brabourne Road would yearn for a management trainee job in those business firms—Andrew Yule, Balmer Lawrie, Bird and Company and Martin Burn, names that have now virtually vanished.

I was completing my final year BSc course, residing at the college hostel. Father de Bonhome, the principal of St Xavier's College, asked me whether I would like to be recommended for a trainee's job at McKinnon McKenzie. It was a fine firm, he could suggest only two from the whole college and the salary would be Rs 450 per month. I calmly said that I was honoured to be recommended; in reality, I was thrilled. I did not consult my father, who had moved to Bombay.

With a borrowed suit and soaring dreams, I was interviewed at the McKinnon office. After being seen by two managers, I saw one Mohi Das, the managing director. He asked me several thoughtful questions. As I was getting convinced that I had done well and might actually get the job, he drew up close to me and asked, 'Son, may I call you that way? Don't get me wrong, but you are just past eighteen. You can have the job; we can train you quite well. But, tell me, do you need the job? How is the family situation?'

I was a little offended, what did my family situation have to do with the job? He clarified, 'Well, I have spent my career in one set of circumstances, but you will spend your career in an entirely different set of circumstances. I feel you should get a professional degree. You can always get this kind of job, son— unless the family situation requires you to get a job right now.'

How could he dangle one of the most prized jobs in front of me and then say what he did? I did not want to listen to him. And I was quite clear about my future (or so I thought) without asking too many people!

Reluctantly, I decided after some thought that I should inform my father of my wish to accept the job. He was furious that I could even think of taking up a job. My dream job ended like a collapsed balloon. I went on to study further and joined Hindustan Lever subsequently.

I never met Mohi Das after that encounter. He retired in due course. A few years ago, I learned that he had died in Coonoor. He would not have recognized this story even if I had had the chance to remind him. He influenced and counselled me about my career by demonstrating deep empathy and in a valuable way, but unknowingly.

Like gentle drops of fine rain that touch you but do not interfere with you, casual advice comes your way. You need to listen to and reflect on them. Then take your own decision. Particularly for a generation that is as blessed as the youth in today's India, this would be wise.

Developing Empathy through an Arabian Experience

I learned another great lesson in empathy some twenty years ago when the Babri Masjid was demolished at Ayodhya on 6 December 1992 (*see* Box 4.3).

For the first time in my life, I was a minority Hindu in a Muslim country, and an explosive situation had developed outside of my control.

Between December 1992 and June 1993, my family went through some extraordinary experiences, through which I

Box 4.3   Tremors from Afar

I used to live in Jeddah to work in Unilever Arabia, a subsidiary of Unilever PLC. My family, comprising my wife and three young children, was with me on the posting. We led a comfortable life in the Arabian Homes expatriate compound and my work was exciting. There were a few restrictions in Jeddah, so we adjusted to life there during the eighteen months preceding December 1992.

What we saw on television on 6 December 1992 in faraway Jeddah was dramatic and unbelievable. Nearly one lakh people had assembled at Ayodhya. Suddenly, a few hundred of the crowd broke through the cordons and attacked the mosque. They clambered on to the domes of the mosque and hoisted saffron flags. They demolished the structure with shovels, iron rods and pickaxes.

You can imagine the commentaries in Jeddah that accompanied the TV reports of this unprecedented incident. It was a mind-blowing, spine-chilling experience. In social circles, the talk was that the Hindus of India had demolished a sacred mosque; the atmosphere was extraordinarily tense.

learned some lessons on empathy. Until then I never understood the oft-debated 'insecurity of the Muslims of India'. I had always argued that the Muslims had religious freedom, equal democratic rights, additional constitutional rights and special political privileges. How can there be any insecurity in their life in India? Merely because Muslims were a 10-12 per cent minority, how it could be argued that they suffered periodic bouts of insecurity?

A few weeks after the unfortunate episode, I received a telephone call from an unknown person. He introduced himself as a well-wisher and recommended that my family and I should depart from the kingdom forthwith as there was danger to our security. According to him, at a discussion in a Riyadh mosque that day, my name had featured as part of a list of non-Muslim Indian citizens who were earning handsome salaries in Saudi Arabia.

The report was plausible as such a list was not difficult to construct—all salary earners had to make a mandatory contribution to GOSI, a government health scheme. You could work out the gross salary backwards from the GOSI contribution. The rhetoric and complaint was that non-Muslim Indians were earning high salaries in the kingdom and diverting their savings to promote a fanatical Hindu organization which was breaking mosques. Before I could ask more questions, the line got disconnected. It was an unnerving experience.

My wife and I were determined not to depart from the kingdom on the basis of an anonymous call. It could have been a crank call. However, I was unclear about what I should do. I spoke to my Unilever director, Roy Brown, in London. Upon his advice, I called on the British Consul General to inform him of the call. Strangely, I did not contact the Indian embassy, which, in hindsight, I should have done.

A few weeks later, my wife mentioned that our car was being followed, always by the same person whose face was hidden behind a checked kafayeh. If our driver approached him, the car would speed away. The stranger was around but never close enough to be asked who he was or why he was following us. My Muslim driver from Kerala confirmed that we were indeed being followed.

I found this disturbing. My wife felt even more insecure as I was travelling to London and Dubai frequently without an adequate contingency plan to meet an ugly situation that might develop in my absence.

Unilever had a long-standing partnership with the well-known and influential Beit Binzagr, the House of Binzagr. I did not wish to be seen as panicking, so I did not mention anything to any of the four brothers of our partner firm.

Once when I was in the government office, I received a call from my wife. It was unusual for my wife to call me unless there was something of importance. This was before the advent of the now ubiquitous cell phones.

She said that the same man had trailed our two daughters all morning and was parked right outside our home. When our driver approached him, he did not drive away. He said that he was not following anybody, so there was no need for irrelevant questions. My wife said that she was very scared to step out of the house. It was a Thursday, and the weekend was ahead.

It was a weekend of anxiety. Although the Babri Masjid matter had quietened down, there had been communal riots in Bombay; there were constant press and television commentaries on the subject. The atmosphere was tense, and it was not at all comfortable to know that one's name may have been mentioned in a mosque or that one might be followed.

Mr Binzagr met the governor and his officials after the weekend. The facts of the story emerged. He could not quite confirm whether my name was mentioned at the Riyadh mosque in December 1992. What he could confirm was that a petition was carried by a group of citizens to the king's periodic majlis. The petition said that ten highly paid non-Muslim Indians were acting to the detriment of Islam and requested that they be sent out of the kingdom forthwith.

The officers concerned argued that merely because these ten people were non-Muslims, it could not be assumed that they were indulging in anti-state or anti-religious activities. Did the agitated petitioners have any specific evidence or complaint? If there was none, the best that the administration could do was to trail them and establish whether they were engaged in prohibited activity. The governors of the provinces were asked to place the ten people under benign surveillance. In this way, the administration defused a potentially incendiary situation from conflagrating.

On the advice of the Binzagrs, my family ignored the man following us. Sure enough, by the end of May, the surveillance stopped and life returned to normal. When I met the Indian ambassador in May, he seemed fully aware of the background. He even wondered why I had not contacted the Indian embassy as the others had done.

During that period, the family saw the experience as a violation of its privacy. The insecurity that my family felt for those six months was nerve-racking. Why? We were a minority among a Muslim majority. Every action or word of ours was liable to a polarized interpretation by a population which believed that Hindus were persecuting Muslims in India. It was not that all Hindus in India were persecuting Muslims, but that was the lens through which we were being seen.

My feeling of empathy developed and, for the first time, I could deeply feel and understand why the Indian Muslim might feel insecure. It was not to do with facts and statistics; it was to do with feeling and emotions. The action of a few might alienate a whole community.

When I was at the receiving end, I felt immediately empathetic! Ever since that experience, I find it easy and desirable to feel for the minority without sitting in judgement or indulging in rhetoric.

It is worthwhile to read the inspiring story of Helen Keller and her teacher Anne Sullivan. It is a classic case of empathy (*see* Box 4.4).

Box 4.4   Blind Empathy

Sometimes we are unable to explain the choice made by somebody. A sense of empathy may help to explain. For example, what made Nehru quit his flourishing legal practice and plunge into India's independence movement? What made Mother Teresa do what she did? Surely it was some emotional episode which aroused a feeling of empathy for a cause. Perhaps that is what they call 'the inner voice'.

There is the touching story of Helen Keller who rose above her disabilities to become internationally famous and help handicapped people lead fuller lives. This is a good illustration of the relationship between two people, built out of a deep sense of empathy.

Helen Keller was afflicted with a serious illness when she was less than two years old. This shut off her ability to see and to speak, and thus her connection to the world. For five years, she grew up, as she later said, 'Wild and unruly, giggling and chuckling to express pleasure, uttering the choked screams of the deaf-mute to express the opposite'. When Helen was seven, her father consulted the Perkins Institution for the Blind in Boston.

A young lady, Anne Sullivan, was deputed from Boston to teach Helen. Anne herself had been nearly blind during her childhood, but a surgery restored her sight partially. Anne cherished and empathized with the value of sight due to her own experience.

There was a great bond of empathy between Anne and Helen. Anne Sullivan was able to make contact with Helen's mind through the sense of touch. Gradually, the child was able to connect words with objects and within three years she knew the alphabet and could read and write in Braille.

Anne Sullivan stayed with Helen Keller for many years. Helen graduated from Radcliffe College with honours in 1904 and went on to devote her life to improving the conditions of the blind and deaf. It is well known that Annie Sullivan was the gifted teacher who unlocked the intelligence of the young, blind and deaf Helen Keller.

Later in life, Anne Sullivan lost her sight. It was Helen Keller who taught her beloved teacher Braille.

Careful Listening: The Need for Self-training

It is remarkable that we are never taught how to breathe or how to listen. Certainly with respect to breathing, there is more and more awareness of lessons on how to breathe properly. With respect to listening, the lessons are few and far between.

The human ear is a strange product of evolution. It is designed to listen well. In practice, perhaps we do not do it too well.[3]

In reptiles, the two-part ear, comprising the inner and the outer, is attached to the jaw. Therefore, when a lizard eats, it cannot speak or hear. So also conversely. Mammals have a three-part ear, an evolutionary innovation. There is an additional middle ear, which is detached from the jaw.

The mammalian ear is a master of detecting very quiet sounds. Yet we humans do not listen too well. Husbands do not listen well to wives, bosses do not listen too well to employees, and parents do not listen too well to their next-gen children.

Yet listening well and reflecting upon what we have listened to is a key part of implicit feedback. How can we listen better? Strangely it seems that the deaf can teach us how to listen better.[4]

Bruno Kahne worked with deaf people and became familiar with their 'silent culture'. He learned five lessons from them which facilitate better interpersonal relationships.

Look people in the eye

Many of us take notes as we listen to people so that we can remember things. Some of us are not fully engaged with the speaker. On the other hand, deaf people look at the speaker in the eye and make sure that they are fully present in the interaction. They absorb more and retain more.

Don't interrupt

In many management situations, and certainly in television debates, there are simultaneous and multiple conversations. That will never happen with deaf people. They follow a strict protocol of one person speaking at a time. Consensus and agreement are reached faster than out of a heated and overlapping conversation. 'In the long term, slower is faster,' writes Kahne.

Say in a simple way what you mean

Deaf people are direct and they communicate with their thoughts and feelings. They tend not to hide behind flowery words. They are economical about the way they communicate. For the same reason, they listen well too.

Ask to repeat if you do not understand

Sign language is evolving much more than the spoken word. New signs evolve all the time. Signs used by people from one region may be different from those used by people from another region. Therefore, deaf people do not hesitate to ask for clarification if they have not understood something.

Be focused

Deaf people do not multitask; they concentrate on the interaction on hand. They cut themselves off from distractions. With the advent of PDAs and Blackberrys, hearing people do the opposite.

Deaf people demonstrate how to exchange information efficiently and without adornment, says Kahne.

Box 4.5
KEY MESSAGES

Since explicit messages and feedback are difficult to come by, you must learn to pick up implicit messages and feedback.

~~~

Empathy is one way of picking up implicit messages. Empathy is the ability to feel the other person's feelings without being judgemental about the legitimacy of those feelings.

~~~

Careful listening is another way of picking up implicit messages and feedback. But nobody teaches us to listen. Observations of how deaf people try to listen offer lessons on better hearing.

PART II

THE INNER WORLD

CHAPTER 5

The Physical Self
Your Only Car

'We should die "young" but as late as possible.'
—Ashley Montagu

The inner world of the manager and leader has three aspects, the sum total of which makes the person who he is and how he will function in his inner world: the *physical* self, the *psychological* self and finally the *ethical* and *spiritual* self.

It is good to begin with the physical self. Fitness and sleep represent huge points of stress to the manager. These days everyone seems to be in a highly charged, time-challenged cauldron.

The Physical Self: Fitness

I doubt that an unfit, stressed chief executive makes a positive impression on the investors or customers of his company. The stereotype shown in advertisements of the high-living and high-spending executive is mythical and is certainly not worthy of emulation.

You can convince yourself about the reasons for not keeping fit—that there is no time to exercise, that it is important to network and socialize, how difficult it is to secure a club membership, problems of timing and logistics and a whole host of other plausible reasons. However, even if all these are true, you can always go for a walk or do yoga.

There are no good enough reasons for lack of fitness and exercise other than indulgence, laziness and procrastination. These bonsai traps take their toll after mid-career.

It is in the first ten years of the working career that the neglect of health begins. Sportsmen stop playing sports, teetotalers drink alcohol, non-smokers smoke, active youngsters sit near-immobile at their desks and starving hostel inmates eat rich food. These early years are the ones to watch.

While growing up in Calcutta, I joined a tennis coaching scheme at the Bengal Lawn Tennis Association. It was run and supervised by Dilip Bose, the Indian Davis Cup tennis star of the 1940s. He was a fiend for fitness. Before we could get our tiny hands around the racket, he would make us run around the South Club tennis courts ten times, skip one hundred times using a skipping rope and do another fifty sit-ups. We were too tired to play any tennis by the time all this was done.

His message was that we could not be tennis players if we were not fit.

One day, Dilip Bose asked us, 'How would you take care of your car if you were told that it would be the only car you would have for your whole life?' In the early 1950s, for a middle-class family in India, there was little hope of ever owning a car, let alone a replacement for an old one! Anyway the answer was self-evident; all the kids said the same thing in chorus.

'Well, your body is the only car you will have for all your life. You cannot change it, so look after it like your only car,' he bellowed.

To a kid, that was a simple message to understand and to remember. I owe it to the late Dilip Bose that I grew to love exercise and tennis, both of which have been an inexhaustible source of pleasure, relaxation, character-building and fitness, all rolled into one.

Upon arrival in Bombay for my first job, an early expenditure was on a membership of the Bombay Gymkhana. The club membership took precedence over the purchase of a motor cycle, music system or occasional fine dining—that too at Bombelli on Warden Road, not the Taj.

It is pleasing to see health-conscious executives exercising and keeping fit. A management career is extremely stressful, and every young executive should work at managing that stress. Some are unlucky because they develop health problems without bringing it upon themselves. But others squander away their good health on the grounds that office work is stressful. Healthy and young people need not develop stressful social habits, deluding themselves that it is relaxing. Such a hectic lifestyle catches up after ten years.

JK was my university tennis partner; he was already a state-level champion when I met him for the first time in the 1960s. I used to wish I had his ground strokes and his swing. When I met JK after forty years, we spoke about tennis. 'Oh, I gave up twenty years ago. I should have taken better care and played more regularly after college. I should have controlled some of my habits. I had to stop after a bypass surgery several years ago,' he said to my great regret.

Many young executives live their life as though exercise and spirituality become relevant only after middle age. Nothing can be further from the truth. The role of exercise and spirituality may increase as you approach middle age, but the seeds of developing these must be sown early in life.

You need not lead a spartan life. Go out and enjoy yourself; youth comes only once. However, do listen to what your body is telling you and do not flog it to capacity. Your good health is an asset on your balance sheet. Grow it, maintain it, but do not destroy it. It is the only opening balance of asset you get at the beginning of your life.

The Physical Self: Sleep

The journalist Patricia Morrisroe writes that we have learned a lot about sleep and insomnia, but we have forgotten how to rest. Insomnia is a unique disorder in that the patient is also the chief diagnostician. Our ancestors huddled together in caves worrying that a tiger or a bear would eat them. We lie down on expensive beds with the most comfortable mattresses, fidgeting with our Blackberries or texting our friends. As the anthropologist Mathew Wolfmeyer noted, 'If a society cannot rest, how can it sleep?'

Late nights, hectic travel and high living are associated with success and, by association, with high performance only in movies, magazines and advertising commercials. In reality, such a lifestyle only delivers stress and sleeplessness. It is incredible how much of a threat lack of sleep is to managerial performance.

Sleep experts opine that if your organization wants to raise managerial productivity and performance, the leaders must pay attention to the issue of managerial sleeplessness.

For young people, lots of fun and a little less sleep over a weekend is understandable. Some executives mistake inadequate sleep with vitality and style. They proudly proclaim how long they work, how they need to socialize until late, and how they manage with only five hours of sleep.

As a general statement of lifestyle, inadequate sleep is a bad idea. It distracts you in a way you are seldom aware of; it creeps upon you imperceptibly. Then there is the bravado of self-importance, about not being able to take a few days' leave. Clubbed together, you have a recipe for disaster—not merely to health, but to judgement.

Sometimes, in the case of successful senior executives with a need for image building, public relations officers and the media eulogize their need for very little sleep. It is probably true for the exception. Each person's physiology is different, and it is plausible that some super-scientist, chairman or software honcho can do with just a few hours' sleep. It is not necessary to behave as though everyone can or should do the same, especially when the other sober habits of these short-sleeping icons are not easy to emulate!

It is as silly to cultivate, or aspire for, managers who sacrifice sleep as it is to groom airline pilots who have had a tipple. Studies have shown that the effects of a week of four to five hours' sleep a night are equivalent to a 0.1 per cent blood alcohol level.

A sleep survey is conducted in America every year. In the 2008 survey conducted by the National Sleep Foundation, it was found that 33 per cent of the working population become very drowsy on the job or actually fall asleep. A 'working person' is defined as one who works over thirty hours a week. By emerging market standards, thirty-three hours of work a week is pitiably low. If such a low level of work suffers from the deleterious effects of sleeplessness, imagine how much worse it could be for those who work over sixty hours a week!

When you are in need of sleep, your skills start to decline. Both visual discrimination and memory slide. As a result, your concentration slides. The opposite happens when you doze off for a while.

Sleep helps people to connect unassociated information which can be used for creative problem-solving. Hence the expression 'Let me sleep over this matter and let us discuss tomorrow'.

Robert Stickgold, associate professor of psychiatry at the Division of Sleep Medicine at Harvard Medical School and Beth Israel Deaconess Medical Center, Boston, has found evidence that important memory processes occur while one sleeps. Naps can help people separate the essentials of an issue from the extraneous detail. He even advocates the deployment of nap rooms by companies and advises them to implement a pro-napping policy.[1]

Animals take short and quick catnaps and do not require long stretches of sleep. It is different with humans. Although some are lucky to feel rested with catnaps, most people are not.

When you are drowsy, several thousand sleep neurons in the brain take over, and you involuntarily lose control. Sometimes, it is for just a few seconds, and one can only hope that you are not driving at that time.

Charles Czeisler, professor at Harvard Medical School, is a leading authority on human sleep cycles and the biology of sleep and wakefulness (*see* Box 5.1). He has observed that top executives have a critical responsibility to take inadequate sleep seriously. Sleep deprivation is not just an individual health hazard, it is a public one.[2]

Lack of Fitness and Sleep Creeps Up on You

Prakash was just thirty when he joined a large company as a mid-career recruit. He was well qualified, had gathered considerable experience in selling and was gregarious and relationship-oriented—all the ingredients that the company sought in its marketing people.

Box 5.1   Sleep Travails

Czeisler lists four sleep-related factors that affect your ability to focus and concentrate. First, for the period that you are awake, namely the duration of the working day, the body builds up a drive to get sleep next. That drive increases with the number of hours you have been awake.

Second, the ability to focus is influenced by the total number of hours of sleep that your body has had for the preceding few days. Beginning the day with a breakfast meeting at 8 a.m. and finishing with a dinner meeting which ends at 11 p.m. for a few days in succession does reduce your ability to focus.

Third is the brain's mechanism that tells the body that it is morning or evening. The technical jargon for this is the brain's 'circadian phase'. This becomes very important with an increasing amount of transcontinental air travel. You are very lucky if you can sleep well on a plane journey, ideally on your own or with a mild sedative. However, too many instances of long distance travel and 'driving directly to the meeting venue from the airport' are not great ways to focus.

The fourth is a related concept called 'sleep inertia'. This is the period it takes a sleeping person to awake. The brain needs time to 'warm up' when you are awakened, a bit like a car engine.

Age has a further influence. Most senior executives tend to be over forty, by which time they have probably gained weight and become more sensitive to external conditions like their bed or the noise around them.

Prakash enjoyed his drink, parties and late nights. He could work incredibly hard through the day. He could also party incredibly hard late into the night. He was a natural business leader, and also a terrific social leader. He would boast that his managers were colleagues at work, but in the evenings they were his friends. Being a competent manager with a strong people's touch, Prakash became a popular friend, a much admired boss and a great team leader.

His bosses appreciated his hard work and his ability to deliver results; his subordinates loved his open style. His peers grudgingly admired his ability to socialize endlessly. Prakash quickly rose in the company and within ten years he was pretty much at the top-leadership level.

Progressively he put on weight and started to slow down perceptibly. His physical appearance left some people wondering whether it was caused by the natural physiological process or whether it was accelerated by his lifestyle. The doubt arose because his energy was boundless and it could mask any tell-tale signs. If he seemed a bit unfocused occasionally, it was assumed that the previous night must have been long, and that he must have hardly caught a few winks; he would perhaps recover by the morrow!

By now, Prakash was running a large division and was taking big decisions. At precisely the time when his judgement was crucial for the business, it became erratic. He developed differences with his boss; he took new product decisions, which went wrong. A number of unexpected business difficulties started to plague the division.

He resented it when these failings were pointed out, as he was convinced that he had a proven track record. Finally, he quit to join another company. Initially, he impressed them with his quick grasp and positive social manners. However, his judgement went wrong again and he moved on from there too.

It is instructive to reflect on why successful executives do not do what is obvious, which is to take enough exercise and get enough sleep. The answer lies in the human tendency to procrastinate and to believe that there will be an opportunity tomorrow to make up for today's indulgences. Procrastination is a subject of academic research.[3]

Researchers have established that people are unrealistic about implementing their intentions about future benefits such as exercise or savings. People put off doing unpleasant things for the future rather than do them today.

That is why good habits are the key to all success. You succeed by keeping fit and healthy, by doing the right things as a matter of practice and from early on.

Be Like a River

My friends joke that all this is easy to say but quite difficult to practise. This is true. Laziness is part of the way we are made and it is our nature to postpone and procrastinate. Bharat Savur, an author, suggests the adoption of the ways of the running river.[4] I do not know if it helps, but it is worth the try. He suggests that you do what a river does.

- Boldly venture on a line of action
- Keep moving
- Overcome the obstacles and blockers
- Follow your trail to the end
- Track your progress
- Initiate a 'no excuse' week for being active.

Here is an example of what Tata Consultancy Services (TCS) does to make it easier for its young workforce to remain fit and healthy.

Why TCS Emphasizes Sports

Tata Consultancy Services, the innovative developer of the offshore delivery model in information technology services, has an employee strength of nearly one and a half lakh. The average age is twenty-seven, and most employees have been educated in engineering or management or both. These young people have a frenetic professional life: they work long hours, often in isolation at the computer terminal, but they are hugely ambitious. They are deeply driven by deadlines.

The high stress level desk job, continuous exposure to the computer screen and the immense concentration required to achieve optimum performance in this competitive environment place a stress on the young executive. In the early 2000s, company leaders were convinced that they needed to address the issue. This prompted the company to seek ways to encourage employees to participate in activities that would make them physically fit and encourage them to take up those activities that they had a passion for before they entered the world of work.

The company started encouraging its employees to participate in sports and outdoor activities. This was done internally through the company's in-house self-help group called Maitree, which organized weekend hikes, setting up of music and dance clubs and volunteering for social causes.

The company set up gymnasiums, tennis courts, squash courts and table tennis facilities at most of its premises and also hired outside facilities for cricket, basketball and football. Dance and yoga instructors were hired. The classes were held in the office premises and often after a session employees would return to work.

Enthusiasm for these activities was generated through word of mouth, internet and peer pressure. The company created a sports portal, accessible to all employees, highlighting sporting achievements and participation, chats, sports news through an outside agency and health-related information.

TCS also ran a campaign to collect a database of sportspersons among its employees, giving details of the various games that they played and their achievements. The company found among its employees international- and state-level players. Owing to various reasons, the chief one being concentration on academics, they had given up their sporting careers.

TCS now has a cricket, football, basketball, badminton, chess and table tennis team in all its offices. The company is proud that its men and women have won several tournaments in these sports.

The company won the group's internal tennis tournament in 2008 and 2009. This must be contrasted to the situation a few years ago when the company struggled to make a team. The tennis programmes are being run effectively by former champions, including Davis Cupper Ramesh Krishnan in Chennai and Illyas Ghouse in Hyderabad. They also hold clinics once a year for the spouses and children of employees.

Running is a good form of exercise, especially for young associates who want to keep fit. The company sponsored the Mumbai marathon. The CEO himself completed the run in his first year of initiation. This served as quite an encouragement to the others. In 2010, the company had nearly forty full marathoners and 180 half marathoners taking part in the Mumbai marathon.

These activities have not only benefited the employees but have also been of great value to their work. They will be fit, more active and confident; their skill in sports gives them the opportunity to be more social wherever they travel or reside.

Through sports, cultural and social activities, employees naturally become better rounded human beings who value the importance of team work, build friendships within and outside the company and gain social skills. Often corporates spend time and money to tutor them in these skills.

TCS is at present actively involved with F1 racing, Mumbai marathon, the Indian Premier League and the National Basketball Association. The company's aim is to extend this to its overseas branches and have internal competitions both within India and overseas so that the associates can interact with each other and develop long-term friendships and camaraderie.

Box 5.2
KEY MESSAGES

You can take your body for granted for a few years.
Lack of fitness and sleep catches up suddenly
and without notice.

The seeds of physical fitness must be sowed
early in life.

There are cases of a few exceptions where lack
of physical fitness or inadequate sleep has not
interfered with intellectual output. It is not wise
to assume that you belong to that category.

CHAPTER 6

The Psychological Self
You Need a Zorba

'Every now and then, take a little relaxation, because when you come back to work, your judgement will be surer. To remain constantly at work will cause you to lose your power of judgement.'—Leonardo da Vinci

This chapter explores the psychological self. The subject of psychology was developed in the western tradition. The western approach is, generally, to break up a problem or issue into its component parts and subject each component to analysis and reason. Such a study leads to an understanding of how the component functions and what its role is in the larger system of which it is a part. Such knowledge leads to an understanding of *how* things work.

The eastern tradition is different. It tends to be holistic and concerns itself with *why* things work. Its approach is to consider the problem or issue as a whole, as a unity, and to appreciate the interplay of the components. It recognizes that the components may play a different role in different circumstances. Hindu philosophy recognizes religion and intuition as a higher form of knowledge, while rationality and sciences are counted as a lower form of knowledge. Chinese philosophy urges an alignment with the Tao, the way, which flows from the unity of opposites, the yin and the yang.[1]

Human behaviour is complex and difficult to understand analytically. Humans are broadly similar from a genetic perspective, yet each individual is distinctive from a psychological perspective. That is why there are no formulaic or prescriptive approaches possible with respect to human relationships, except for the general awareness and recognition that each person is different.

There are opposite forces that determine a person's psychological response to a given situation; they need to be in balance. Such a balance can be found through a release mechanism of 'letting go'. As the epitaph of the Greek author Nikos Kazantzakis in Herakleion reads, 'I hope for nothing. I fear nothing. I am free.'

Kazantzakis wrote the novel *Zorba the Greek*. He created the character called Zorba, one of the greats of modern fiction. The book was later made into a fine film starring Anthony Quinn. It is a story about the relationship between two men.

One is 'The Boss' who has the looks, intelligence, health, money and education. He is a lignite miner with his eye set on prosperity and wealth. He is a good person, but is all locked up inside, a bit like the modern business manager. He does not enjoy life. He reads and thinks, but has no fun.

Zorba is his assistant in the lignite venture. Zorba is a very different person from 'The Boss'. Zorba is fun-loving and takes each incident and day as it comes. Towards the end of the story, Zorba tells his boss, 'You have got everything, Boss, except one thing—madness. A man needs a little madness or he never cuts the rope and gets free.' At the end of the book, Zorba teaches the Boss to let go, dance and laugh.

Managers are like 'The Boss'. They take themselves far too seriously. They need to let go sometimes and for that they need a Zorba in their careers and lives. A Zorba serves as a lightning rod. Someone needs to help you to view your psyche as a balance between your inherent strong points and weak points without getting into professional counselling.

This means learning about three things which cause unhappiness and imbalances in the psyche of the manager: first, learn to cope with 'unfairness'; second, learn to enjoy how you earn a living; third, find the time to let go.

Learn to Cope with Unfairness

An item that appears at the top of every manager's list of reasons for stress is the 'unfairness of the system'—poor feedback, inadequate career development, wrong promotions and so on. The challenge is not to wish away the so-called unfairness, but to learn how to cope with the stress sensibly. This requires a reflective mindset rather than a judgemental one. The story of Karan and Gulab is typical and it occurs all the time in every company at various levels.

Karan and Gulab were highly regarded business leaders; both were contenders for a senior-level job in their company. Both were accomplished and had put in long years. When the time came, the board decided that Karan should be promoted. The dilemma was how to tell Gulab. At a delicate meeting with Gulab, the directors explained their difficulty in coming to a decision and informed him they had finally decided upon Karan.

Gulab's world crashed—the prized job he had worked for all his life was not to be his. His throat choked, tears almost spilled out of his eyes and there was a storm raging in his heart. 'After all these years of what I have done for this company,' he thought.

'Well, we have said what we have to,' continued the directors calmly. 'Please understand that it was difficult for us to make a choice. There could well be another opportunity for you in the future. Please do not think of leaving the firm.'

Gulab was livid. An instinct guided him to cope through reflection rather than become judgemental. He addressed the directors: 'During my career, I too have had to make choices about managers at levels below mine and have had to counsel the disappointed colleague. I have worked here because I felt this company to be fair; I cannot suddenly change that view. However, you can be fallible. In this case, I feel that you are making a big mistake. You would expect me to feel so, hence I will not elaborate. You have made a choice as fairly as you could. I thank you for your advice to avoid haste. I will continue to work for some time and will think through my next course of action.'

Gulab was crushed emotionally and, in such a situation, even the most reasonable person can become unreasonable. He was convinced that the system had been unfair to him. He could see no sense or logic whatsoever in the choice made by his superiors. Gulab's wife turned out to be his Zorba, his pillar of strength. She brought up alternative ways of viewing the issue, some to his indignation and annoyance. She persisted in pointing out that fairness has a large element of perception. She encouraged him to solve the right question: Did he have a happy future in this company? It was not whether he had been treated fairly or not.

That is what Gulab did. He could deal with the issue calmly because he listened to his Zorba; he placed himself in the shoes of those who had to decide. He allowed himself the time to think things through.

He continued to work diligently but progressively became unhappy with the way events developed. Instead of cribbing, he found an alternative way to restore his happiness, that is, a suitable opportunity elsewhere. He moved on to a new life. Most importantly, he retained warm ties with his old colleagues, and left with fond memories of the good times he had had while working in that company.

Enjoy How You Earn a Living

We can have fun only if we see fun in the work we do and the people we work with. Managers must learn to enjoy their work and career. The fact that you encounter problems and difficult people during the course of your work is part of the fun. 'Life is a series of problems. Do you want to moan about them or solve them?' the author Scott Peck asks.[2]

While managers need to cope with stress, they must also learn to have fun, because it is a lightning rod for stress. The noted sports writer Harsha Bhogle is a management graduate. Addressing professional managers, he once argued that he had made his passion his job, while most managers try to make their jobs their passion.

A career means different things to different people. To some, it is an end point: it is a statement of ambition. For instance, I must become the CEO of this company. To others, it means the landmarks on the way; I must become regional manager in two years and general manager in three years thereafter. To most, it is a combination. However, these are all destinations and not the journey.

To the wise, it means the enjoyment and experiences of work. A career is not a destination; a career is the journey.

So what kind of a journey must you have? The answer is a journey which you enjoy. You can excel with consistency only at tasks you enjoy. Conversely, you cannot excel with consistency at tasks that you do not enjoy. Enjoyment does not mean that the task is easy, or that you know how to do it; it is in fact quite the reverse.

You enjoy doing things that challenge you sufficiently, that engage you and are instructive, for instance, selling to a difficult customer, debugging a production issue or configuring a least-cost solution to a problem. You may find it engaging, but some may hate the same tasks.

During the 1980s a young manager, DL, joined the corporate communications department of Hindustan Lever. He had gone to an excellent school, had a fine degree from a great college, was intelligent and articulate, and had cleared a series of tough company interviews. He was a creative writer and had all the characteristics of becoming a successful manager. However, recruiting and developing managers based on externally visible characteristics is fraught with risk.

One of the preparatory tasks before DL could be assigned his first responsibility was field training. He had to work on a salesman's beat with an experienced salesman for sixteen weeks. This involved visiting grocery shops and booking orders all day long. The idea was for him to learn the routine, pains and tribulations of a salesman.

DL was miserable. He found it boring; in fact, he called it 'demeaning'. After spending some time with him, his boss wondered whether DL would ever make a good sales manager. That did not per se make him a good or a bad manager; it just meant that DL had to rethink what kind of work he should do to enjoy himself. The Hindustan Lever job was quite a prized one: getting such a job was prestigious; conversely, not being successful was considered a negative by many.

As DL thought about it, something kept telling him that he had joined Hindustan Lever just to prove to the world how smart he was; the salary was a huge added attraction. It was not that he understood this career and he wanted to try it.

What he truly enjoyed was spending time with school students—telling them about things they did not know, and some things that they might never know. He wanted to be a school teacher!

Implementing his idea meant sacrificing his salary and his image among his family members and peers. He was courageous and took the plunge by quitting one of the most prized jobs of that time.

I met him twenty years later. By then, he was the headmaster of a prestigious public school, probably earning a fraction of what he might have if he had stayed on at the company. He was enjoying himself, doing all sorts of new things in the school and that gave him a sense of satisfaction. He told me that he had found his calling, his journey had been exciting and he looked forward to each day as the sun rose.

DL had understood what a career meant—doing what you enjoy and enjoying what you do. DL had realized that what was important was the journey, not the destination.

Find the Time to Let Go

There are many career dynamos whom you can see all around your workplace. They are overzealous managers who feel so important that they have not found it possible to take a holiday almost throughout their career. They have weeks and weeks of accumulated leave when they retire. On the few occasions when they have gone on leave, they are in touch with the office through various means of communication. They bark out orders while sunning themselves on the beach or as they enter a theatre for a show with the family. God take care of them!

Talking for myself, I have been indulgent in this respect throughout my career. I cannot recall even one year when I could not be spared some time to go on holiday. Not once has any boss—and I have had about fifteen bosses in over four decades—asked me whether I needed the leave or could I please cancel my planned holiday. Where do these officious managers find their bosses? I wonder.

To sum up, the three biggest sources of unhappiness among corporate executives, in my experience, stem from not being able to cope with unfairness, not enjoying what you do in your job, and not finding the time to let go.

What about the positive side of the coin? What makes for the happiness of an individual?

What Makes Us Happy?

There is a fine essay based on what must be the world's most comprehensive and long-standing piece of research on the subject of what makes us happy, the famous 'Grant study' by George Valliant.[3] Valliant began with 240 high-performing Harvard graduates of the classes of 1942–44. He tracked them for over sixty years from their college days through to their eighties.

It is the most exhaustive research and represents a lifetime of commitment by Valliant. The candidates are mostly anonymous, but the study included famous people like John F. Kennedy and Ben Bradlee, editor of the *Washington Post*.

The results would be familiar to anybody who has studied eastern philosophy, particularly the Bhagavad Gita. The findings are fascinating as they are placed in a modern context.

Here is a practical answer to the questions 'What makes people happy? What allows people to work and love as they grow old?'

Valliant identified the seven factors that help individuals to age healthily, both physically and psychologically. Two of them are technical and need some explanation: the use of mature adaptations and building stable relationships. Both these are listed as positive virtues to be cultivated.

Mature adaptation means a wise deployment of adaptations to difficult or tricky situations. If your boss is not appreciative of your work, you need to adapt to the situation. The way you do it when you are less experienced is very different from the way you do it when you are more experienced. The latter will be a more mature adaptation.

Everyone uses defences to cope with the difficulties that will inevitably confront them. These are called 'adaptations'. Early in life, we tend to deploy 'immature' adaptations. As we grow older, we handle difficulties with the wise deployment of defence adaptations. This is what Valliant means when he refers to 'mature adaptations'. Even at an elderly age, some people consistently use 'immature' adaptations. They reduce their chances of being happy.

Valliant also writes about the power of relationships. Warm connections are necessary—from parents, spouse, siblings and friends to mentors. Of the men who were thriving at the age of sixty-five, 93 per cent had been close to a brother, sister or cousin. 'The only thing that really matters in life is your relationship with other people,' Valliant says.

The five factors for ageing healthily and in good psychological state as identified in the study are having a good education, avoiding smoking and abuse of alcohol, doing regular exercise and maintaining correct weight. You may wonder whether you need a study over decades to establish these simple truths. You do. The message is worth testing, proving and emphasizing repeatedly, for managers never seem to practise what they know. That is why these appear as a lesson in the earlier chapter. Indeed your body is the only car you will ever have.

Happiness is the new buzzword.[4] 'Men are no happier than women and people in sunny climates are no happier than those in chilly places. Beautiful people are no happier than ugly people and successful people are no happier than less successful people.' Happiness books and happiness seminars are among the fastest-growing businesses. But it all comes back to sound common sense. Happiness is tied to giving rather than taking, to volunteering, to having a happy marriage and to being connected with siblings and people.

Box 6.1
KEY MESSAGES

Balance is the key to understanding your
psychological self. The balance is between
opposite demands.

———

Having someone (a Zorba) who can teach you
not to take yourself too seriously will help you
avoid career hazards.

———

Coping with unfairness is a common hazard
in a career.

———

Earning a living without enjoyment is the
second hazard.

———

Not finding the time to let go is the third hazard.

———

Adaptability and relationships constitute a
vigorous path to happiness.

CHAPTER 7

The Ethical and Spiritual Self
Direction not Distance

'Beware of politics without principles, wealth without work, pleasure without conscience, education without character, commerce without morality, science without humanity and worship without sacrifice.'—Mahatma Gandhi

Many managers spend a lot of their working time thinking about how to accelerate their promotions, how to be one up on their colleagues while impressing the boss and how to earn money faster. The management world is indeed very competitive. So if you feel that time must be spent thinking through such matters and taking appropriate action, well, you are correct, but only in part.

The question to ask is whether it is the aim of a career to go far or to go in the right direction. Ideally, of course, you should achieve both, but trade-offs do occur all the time.

If you watch club-level golfers, you will see the point. Some stand on the tee box with the longest club and whack the ball with the might of an ox. They are the ones who want to see the ball soar away with an accelerating speed. A few seconds later, when they observe where the ball has landed, they curse and crib. The ball has perhaps been lost or has landed in a difficult spot from which it will be difficult to play the next shot. Other golfers take a measured approach of landing the ball on the fairway at a spot where they want it to land. For them, the next stroke is as important as the first tee shot. Both are valid ways to play the game. If you are talented, you may learn to do both, that is, go far as well as land where you want. Many club-level golfers never achieve this.

The purpose of a career is to utilize your potential fully, whether you are a chairman or an assistant, because only that can give you satisfaction and a sense of self-esteem. It becomes possible to achieve such satisfaction when you are surrounded by friendship and trust, which are essential for the accomplishment of managerial tasks (*see* Box 7.1). That nobody can do a management job all by himself is a well-known fact. It

---

Box 7.1   Wonderful Friends

There was a fine movie, *It's a Wonderful Life*, by Frank Capra starring James Stewart and Donna Reed. The story is about a man who thinks he is a failure. So he prepares to commit suicide.

An angel is sent to prevent his act and to rescue him. The angel finds that the man lacks self-esteem and hence he thinks that his friends and relations do not much care for him. The angel takes him in an invisible form to overhear what his friends and relations think of him in reality. He is surprised that he seemed to be loved by them all and that he mattered to them. His own perception of his failures in his career and business activities bothered them little, and their love for him was overwhelming. He feels blessed.

The message of the film is that no man who has friends is a failure.

Well, it is the same with your career. You take your own successes too seriously, and your failures the same way. Other people do not think about either with the same intensity—they have better things to do!

is the web of relationships and friendships that enables a manager to navigate the choppy waters that the ship of his career will constantly encounter.

Philosophers say that a good question to ponder over is who will come to your funeral when you die. When a loved man dies, lots of people attend his funeral out of choice. When a rich or powerful man dies, lots of people may attend, only because they want to be seen to have been there.

Jon Huntsman started his chemicals firm, Huntsman Corporation, in 1970. Within thirty years, he had built it into the world's largest privately held chemical company. In an elegant book he wrote about the values he thought laid the foundation of his business,[1] he narrates a story about Charles Miller Smith, whom I knew as a Unilever director from my earlier days.

In 1999 Huntsman Corporation and ICI (of which Charles had become CEO) were in deep negotiations regarding the sale of one of the chemical divisions of ICI. Charles desperately needed to get a good price to rescue ICI from its heavy debt and Jon had a limited amount of money for the acquisition. The negotiations were friendly but fierce.

When 80 per cent of the deal had been agreed, Jon's team was confident that they could claw out another $200 million from the price. It was then that Jon learned that Charles's wife was a terminal cancer patient and that Charles was a little preoccupied. She passed away when the deal had not yet been finalized.

Jon Huntsman writes of his affirmative decision to finalize the deal as it was, whether he was losing $200 million or not. He felt that the personal emotional price that would be extracted from Charles would not give Jon any peace. According to Jon, Charles and he are lifelong friends.

If you aim in the right direction, the best possible distance will come automatically. That is a simple truth.

Do Things Right, Not Just the Right Things

Young managers are taught to think that they should take charge of their careers, that they should purposefully plan what they wish to be, what milestones they should achieve and by when. In reality, it is completely different. There are more factors that are out of your control than within. This does not mean that all planning is useless, but this does leave many managers in an anxious state.

Your career goal is *your* statement of intent and desire. The company you work for, the boss's judgement of your work, your seniors' views on your potential, the opportunity that develops in the wider economy—all these have a strong influence. Your own plan has only a limited influence.

Once you recognize and, more importantly, accept this, you can start to do things right rather than do the right things. There is a difference.

Doing the right things means planning a desired outcome for each action or initiative. Doing things right means to stretch and do your best and leave the results to turn out the way they will. I am fond of a story that could be anyone's experience. I had narrated this story in my earlier book, *The Case of the Bonsai Manager*, but I am repeating it here. It is about an iconic and contemporary American business leader.

Dave is the chairman of a large American corporation. When I met him, he told me a story about his career.

He was a young accountant in General Electric some twenty-five years ago. He was working three levels below the chief financial officer, who in turn reported to the legendary chairman,

Jack Welch. One of Dave's tasks was to compile a statement of the company's forward projection of sales and profits—by year, by country and by business unit.

It was a mass of numbers and young Dave could not imagine of what use it could be to anyone. He inquired about its utility from his senior managers, but was advised to do what he had been assigned. The statement was being produced for many years, so would he please continue?

The chairman was trying to tear down the bureaucratic culture of a very traditional company. He had, as is well known, acquired the label 'neutron' to symbolize his bombarding the company with his change agenda. One day the chairman received this complex statement, showing the company's five-year projection of sales and profits.

The chairman was incensed, so he called for the young man who was 'producing this rubbish'. A nervous Dave appeared before him and was too awed to answer the obvious question. He was sent packing with the admonition 'smart guys like you should not do this kind of thing'. Presumably, the CFO's department was hauled over the coals, and Dave received confirmatory instructions to stop the compilation soon thereafter.

Dave wondered why his seniors had brushed aside his question on the same matter, and responded with logic and alacrity to the chairman's hollering! Perhaps you have had such an experience in your workplace.

At a company reception a few months later, the chairman was surrounded by his officers. He noticed young Dave lurking around. He summoned him and inquired whether he had stopped compiling that useless statement. One of the seniors present interjected that it was Dave who had asked questions about the futility of such a statement.

'But you never told me that earlier,' said a surprised chairman. Dave looked shy and remained silent.

Some weeks later Dave's big boss, the CFO, gave Dave a double promotion and applauded his courage in not letting down his team under the chairman's pressure. Of course, Dave was very competent. To his surprise, this unplanned episode told others about his character, which was not at all what Dave was trying to highlight. Character is such an intangible, yet important, part of a leader's qualities. Dave's career advanced in GE and he went on to become the chairman of another company.

So, while you do things right rather than do only the right things, remember that character is as important as competence. The world has enough competent people, but not enough managers with character.

Lead in the Same Way That You Would Like to Be Led

An important border that every manager has to cross is from being a functional manager to being a leader of men. Many underestimate this transition, often to their disadvantage.

You succeed as a functional manager by demonstrating superior knowledge, by using factors within your control to achieve and by working pretty much through your own agenda. In a job 'across the border', you are working with people who know more than you. You can do little by yourself; you depend on others to achieve targets.

You are a leader of men and facing the true test of a general manager.

Hemant had steadily risen within the finance and support functions of a large pharmaceuticals company. He had impeccable credentials as a UK-qualified chartered accountant and an alumnus of the London School of Economics. One day he was promoted as the general manager of a key business unit. He now bore responsibility for sales, marketing, purchasing and other functions.

The medical representatives (MR) in his organization had significant competitive advantage over peers in the industry. They had nurtured the precious relationships with the profession and trade. Although the industry norm was to keep MRs as members of an external union, it was not so in his company. It was important to maintain it that way by being sensitive to their problems.

Hemant's predecessors had risen up from the field or through marketing. He reckoned that the sales force would be apprehensive about having a finance person as their boss. He decided to meet the MRs and understand their problems.

During his early meetings, he learned that the MRs had to perform demeaning and non-professional chores for their bosses. Autocracy, bordering on the indiscriminate use of power, was rampant. To him, this was an issue of ethics! He was outraged.

Being of a calm and reflective nature, Hemant decided not to react immediately or show his disapproval. As he worked his way through meetings with area sales managers and regional sales managers, he found that a similar practice existed in the chain of command right up to the general sales manager. He could hardly fire the whole team, nor could he antagonize any one of them by pointing an accusatory finger.

In a private meeting with his top sales team, he shared his pain. In his twenty years, his bosses had never treated him that way, nor did he expect similar behaviour. How could people not respect the dignity of others in the sales system? After a few meetings, it became clear that this route would not work.

Worse still, his top colleagues saw nothing wrong with their current ways. They genuinely felt that it was a good way to manage and that any softness would be damaging. They rationalized that autocratic discipline was necessary to manage a dispersed group. Some experienced managers felt that the youngsters had to 'go through the mill' as they themselves had done.

Hemant finally resorted to tackling his middle managers. He got them to debate the shared values that they would like to see in the company. When they did this, 'respect for people' featured strongly. Now it was easier for Hemant to suggest, 'If that is the value you people want, let us go out and practise it uniformly!'

There followed a period of persistence and patience. The tough bit was giving marching orders to those who did not fall in line. Finally, the full team, including the senior sales managers, began to see Hemant's point about 'respect for employees'. It took three years of hard work to dismantle the iniquitous system.

Hemant's persistence and faith in relying on values had paid off. He worked through the problem and persuaded people instead of being moralistic or evangelical or, worse still, falling into the trap of ordering them to do as he felt.

You have to lead your people, not as you were led earlier in your career, but as you would want to be led in the future. You do not seek applause, but you may get applauded.

Leadership Is Based on Courage

Management is about leadership—of people, of ideas, of markets. It is not merely about how far you go, and definitely not about doing what you are told to do; it is about doing what you are paid to do. Managers need to remind themselves about this eternal truth.

Courage is not just another leadership quality like intelligence, compassion and determination. In reality, it is the iron ladder on which all the other virtues sit. Without this iron ladder of courage, other virtues will not be effective.

The quality of this ladder of courage is determined and defined by you; it is what you live by.

Courage is not only for the CEO or the iconic top layer; courage is about everyday things done by managers through an organization. The story of a senior manager, Praveena, is instructive.

At Praveena's retirement function, her colleagues had assembled for a company dinner in the usual manner. The evening programme was progressing predictably. When the speeches began, I thought to myself, 'This will be predictable.'

Praveena first said the usual stuff—gratitude to her colleagues, apologies to those she had offended inadvertently and promises to keep in touch. Suddenly, Praveena's speech changed:

As you know, my role for several years has been to coordinate capital sanctions. Many of you have probably felt that I asked too many questions and retarded the speed of capital expenditure. I have made known my view that, in recent years, we as managers had become lax with regard to capital expenditure. We want to spend quickly, but later, we write off. We install equipment and then fail to use it the way we had planned to.

Cash is the most important resource in any company, and we all know that our company gobbles cash for capital expenditure. My career may have suffered because I was perceived to slow down expenditure. But I feel satisfied that due to my efforts, along with all of you, the company saved Rs xxx crores of valuable cash in the last five years. If this money had been allowed to be spent more easily, we might have Rs xxx crores less cash and, who knows, I may have advanced another level in my career! For me, that is a contribution I am proud of. I am satisfied that I acted in a particular way because I was paid to do so.

She sat down—there were a few seconds of silence and then a round of thunderous applause.

If we analyse her speech in the format of academic thinkers,[2] Praveena demonstrated the power of the CPWRR formula—candour, purpose, will, rigour, risk—in the discharge of her everyday duties.

Candour means the quality of speaking out in a constructive and contributing way. Speaking out in a criticizing and carping way is unproductive.

Purpose is about pursuing lofty and ambitious goals. Praveena realized that her industry was a cash guzzler, that even at her level within the company she could contribute to the judicious usage of cash. She could have taken the easy option of leaving it to her bosses.

Will is the ability to inspire optimism. Will is adding energy to the role you are playing. Praveena did both, she did not merely ask 'clever' questions, she placed alternatives on the table.

Rigour means the discipline to put a process in place. Praveena insisted that the justification for expenditure should follow a predetermined format. In the process, she was perceived as bureaucratic.

Risk is the willingness to trust others to do their bit, while accepting the consequences of your own actions.

It is not enough to have three or four of the above CPWRR. All five need to work together, like the cylinders of an engine.

Box 7.2
KEY MESSAGES

You have to do what is right without appearing
self-righteous. Learn to disagree without
becoming disagreeable.

⎯

Leadership requires you to display courage of
conviction and matching action.

⎯

Do not lead in ways by which you would not
like to be led.

PART III

THE WORLD OF PEOPLE

CHAPTER 8

Connecting
Saying What You Mean

'We cannot make another person change his or her steps to an old dance, but if we change our own steps, the dance can no longer continue in the same predictable pattern.'—Harriet Lerner, *The Dance of Anger*

The 'world of people' means communicating with those around you.

Your world has many people with many ideas and your world view is shaped by what you see and what you believe in. Multiple images and views about matters are an inevitable part of life. Luckily your brain is wired to sort out these contradictory images and views into what is coherent for you. That is how you can live your life with sanity!

The human brain is the most evolved among all living species. It is capable of expressing complex emotions (*see* Box 8.1). Human beings are capable of suppressing an experienced emotion, and outwardly expressing an opposite emotion.

For example, if you do not quite like your neighbour or enjoy your neighbour's company, you would rather not spend time with such a person. Yet you are perfectly capable of having a pleasant conversation with your neighbour in the building elevator and of warmly inviting him or her for an evening drink or a cup of tea.

Human beings are the only species equipped with the hardware to suppress feelings and to express the opposite of their real feelings deliberately. One of the forms this takes is the power of silence.

Silence can take many forms in corporate life. You may keep silent about your real view during a discussion. Later you may make a cynical comment to signal your opposition or even actively subvert any attempt at implementation. Alternatively, you may actually indicate your positive support, though your

---

Box 8.1   The Evolving Brain

Paul MacLean, chief of brain evolution and behaviour at the National Institute of Mental Health in the USA, called the brain a triune—a three in one. Reptiles, the earliest species, have a simple, single part brain. As mammals evolved, an additional layer developed into a dual or two part brain. With further evolution came the human brain, which has three parts.

In the simple part of the brain, basic life functions are supported—breathing, heartbeats, etc. Without proper functioning of this part, life functions would cease. Then evolved an overlay, which is the second part called the paleo-mammalian brain. This supports basic emotions such as fear, hunger and love. When a dog loves you, that expression is evident in the way the dog looks at you. A lizard cannot look at you lovingly!

The third and most evolved part is the neo-cortex, which is very well developed in humans. This holds two uniquely human capabilities: the first is the power of logical and rational thinking and the second is the capability of expressing 'complex' emotions. Complex emoting is the ability to express an emotion which you do not actually feel or experience.

Box 8.2   The Galapagos Company

The Galapagos Islands are 1000 kilometres from the coast of Ecuador. The islands became famous after Charles Darwin visited them in the 1830s. From his observations, he formulated his thesis about evolution. One of the things that Darwin noticed was the fearlessness of the animals; they were tame. Darwin would stride up to giant tortoises and sit on their back. He picked up marine iguanas and tossed them into the ocean. All the birds came so close that Darwin thought he could hit them with his hat.

Why are the birds so fearless? The accepted view is that on islands, as distinct from continents, animals tend to be more fearless. Islands are usually safer places to live and are home to fewer predators like cats and mammals. So the animals there have less fear about becoming someone's lunch.

Companies should create an environment similar to the Galapagos Islands if employees are to speak up and be fearless.

real view is the opposite. Basically silence is practised out of fear (*see* Box 8.2).

Such behaviour has a huge impact on how you connect with the world of people. This has been the subject of study and research in the corporate sector using the field observational tools of an anthropologist. I have derived useful ideas from the Harvard Business School professor Leslie Perlow's book on her observations and work.[1]

Common sense and observation tells you that every manager most likely believes that his interpersonal relationship with co-workers is superior to that enjoyed by his peers. One manifestation of such a belief is that every manager believes that he communicates with directness and openness, but those around him do not. Every manager states that he would like open communication. But when he receives it and the message is negative or damaging, he feels that the giver of the communication has been insensitive. As a result, the giver of the communication deliberately tries to be ambiguous and circumlocutory. To do the opposite requires you to be fearless. In the field of performance appraisal, in particular, this behaviour shows up regularly.

The anecdote about Pratap that follows illustrates an experience many readers must have experienced.

Frank Speak Produces a Negative Cycle

The most common complaint heard in company corridors pertains to the company's appraisal system and the quality of feedback to the manager from his superior. Whatever is done, it never seems good enough. Improving on this aspect is a constant effort everywhere, all the time.

The theoretical characteristics of the ideal appraisal system are known. The feedback message must contain comments with examples and suggestions for improvement. The message must be delivered in a positive environment, a context of trust. Implementing this correctly is complicated.

Thirty-five-year-old Pratap used to work in my department. He was a competent engineer and could solve technical problems reliably. He had two characteristics: first, he was forever critical of other colleagues and departments; second, he was supremely confident that he could run a business. I often wished he would be more realistic. I even hinted as much to him, bearing in mind that he was also a very sensitive individual.

In the natural course of our careers, he and I moved to other parts of the company. We began to work together again after several years. By this time, there was a senior manager between his position and mine. Pratap would drop in occasionally for a chat. Most of the time he would inquire about the family and talk of our earlier work experiences, and I would spend some social time with him.

On one such occasion, Pratap complained that his immediate boss was ambiguous in giving him a performance feedback. As a result, he felt that he was not being considered for advancement into general management. He felt aggrieved. I told him that his boss would give him more direct feedback.

When I broached the subject with Pratap's boss, he insisted that he had given his feedback, which was admittedly delicate, as he did not wish to damage Pratap's self-esteem by being too direct. However, he agreed to try once again. His boss had felt that Pratap's execution capability was limited by his inability to get along with peers and staff from other departments. As a result, his boss felt that Pratap had become part of the problem, not part of the solution.

After three weeks, Pratap arrived in my office in a rather depressed condition. He said his boss had been brutal in his feedback and surely there was no need to make a big deal out of one's supposed shortcomings! I was amazed. I could not help pointing out that he himself had sought a more direct feedback.

'Of course that is true. But that does not mean that you make me feel inadequate or isolated,' he insisted. I found it difficult to agree with him, particularly because Pratap's boss was regarded in the company as one of the most humane and caring managers. I suggested to Pratap that perhaps he was not really ready for a direct feedback.

'But what is your view? You have known me for long,' he persisted. I said that I had participated in the appraisal and concurred with the comments. Pratap was crestfallen. 'Well, I have to think about my future,' he said remorsefully as he left my room.

Pratap left the company and worked in a couple of other companies. Since he was in touch with me for advice and counselling, I could observe that he was not achieving as much happiness as he had expected and, therefore, not much success. All managers say that they want frank and open feedback. Most are unprepared for it. The best feedback is obtained not from what is stated explicitly, but from what is not stated.

If you receive feedback which is ambiguous, it is possible that it is the other person's inherent style. There is not much you can do about that. On the other hand, it is quite possible that the other person is unsure of your preparedness for direct feedback. In this situation, you can do something about it.

In either case, if a manager can learn to listen to the tune behind the actual words, he will get the feedback without damaging his ego and self-esteem. It is a skill to be cultivated.

Frank Speak Produces a Positive Cycle

In chapter 6, we saw Gulab having to adapt after missing an opportunity for promotion. A lesson can be derived by reverting to that anecdote and tracing Gulab's journey after he was told that he would not get the leadership job that he had aspired for.

Having missed the promotion, Gulab waited to assess whether the statement made to him by his directors would work out, that 'there could well be another opportunity, so please do not leave the company'. Obviously there had been no commitment, so he had to wait and see.

After several months, Gulab found himself increasingly bothered about his disagreement and discomfort. The way the company was progressing under Karan's leadership was not in line with Gulab's thinking. He was in a catch-22 situation. If he expressed his views openly, it could be interpreted as a case of sour grapes and poor team play on his part. If he did not express his views, he was not living up to the professional standards that he had set for himself.

Gulab decided to express his views with forthrightness, but took special care to be polite and constructive. His instinct told him that he was not being taken seriously and that he had to move out of his current work relationships. He decided to test the waters directly with his bosses.

He sought out two very senior officers at headquarters. Both were well disposed to Gulab, but were also known to be frank. In their individual ways, each of them separately told Gulab the lay of the land. To Gulab, the message was that he was no longer seen in the same positive way that he had been earlier in his career. The constructive directness of the two conversations helped him reflect and review his career.

Without grief or emotion, Gulab figured that restoring his happiness lay solely in his own hands. He would have to change the relationships and ambience of his work, and if that meant leaving the firm, he would do so.

As mentioned earlier, Gulab did change his job with grace. He restored his happiness through his role in the new company. Unlike Prakash, who carried his unhappiness into new circumstances, Gulab left his unhappiness behind. He created his happiness afresh in his new environment. The directness of his bosses helped him, whereas the same directness did not help Prakash.

The lesson from the two episodes is that people will say 'yes' when they mean 'yes' only when they feel that the recipient genuinely wants the true message.

Silence in Matrimony

It is important to recognize that silence is fundamentally detrimental. Only if you accept this view can you begin the search for a way to be constructively open. This is as true of a marriage as it is about a business situation.

In judging a divorce case in 2010, the Supreme Court of India opined that the silence of a partner could amount to cruelty under Section 13 of the Hindu Marriage Act. In his judgement, Justice A.K. Ganguly wrote, 'In a matrimonial relationship, cruelty would obviously mean absence of mutual respect and understanding between spouses which embitters the relationship and often leads to various outbursts of behaviour that can be termed cruel.'[2]

Silence at Toyota

Defects in automobiles and consequent recalls by manufacturers have been part of auto folklore (*see* Box 8.3).

In early 2010 business papers and magazines carried dramatic news about the Japanese automaker Toyota and

---

Box 8.3   Recalling Cars

In 1971 General Motors had to recall almost 7 million cars. In 1972, Volkswagen recalled 3 million Beetles. In 1987 Ford recalled 4 million vehicles. In 2003 there was a tragic accident in Japan. While walking home with her two young sons from a neighbourhood store in Hiroshima, twenty-nine-year-old Shiho Okamoto was struck by a wheel flying off the front axle of a Mitsubishi truck. Fuso, the heavy trucks division of Mitsubishi, was investigated by the police. They found that there was a systematic attempt by Fuso to hide the fact that almost one million vehicles had been released with a defect. Transport Minister Nobuteru Ishihara said, 'I am so disgusted that I am speechless.'

defective Toyota cars, which accelerated on their own. How could the world's most admired auto company have sent defective cars into the market? There were different angles to the story, but a streak of silence and secretiveness seemed to pervade the denouement of events.

In 2002 the Toyota Camry featured an innovation with respect to the gas pedal. Instead of the traditional mechanical connection of the pedal to the engine, a new technology was implemented where electronic sensors were used to send signals to the computer controlling the engine. Later the technology was extended to the Lexus. The benefit was higher fuel efficiency.[3]

Within a couple of years, the National Highway Traffic Safety Administration (NHTSA) started receiving complaints that some Toyota cars were speeding up without the driver touching the accelerator pedal and by 2006 there were several hundreds of complaints.

The NHTSA is staffed and organized in such a way that it works on the principle of open disclosure and trust. Without transparent self-disclosure by the automaker, there is no way that the Office of Defects can discharge its functions. In this sense, the auto industry is almost self-regulated.

The heart of Toyota's accelerating pedal problem was traced by commentators to its secretive culture. *The Economist* commented, '. . . they have a rigid system of seniority and hierarchy in which people are reluctant to pass on bad news up the chain, thus keeping information from those who need to hear it in a misguided effort to protect them from losing face'.

This culture clashes with the American requirement that automakers disclose safety threats. Despite Toyota having operated in the United States since 1957, the top leadership had few American executives. Leaders lived in Japan and communicated in traditional terms.

Finally the NHTSA was fed up with the slowness of Toyota information flow. The leadership in Toyota also changed and the secret was out soon: the Toyota headquarters officers had known for some time that there was a defect in the pedal. Over 2.3 million Toyota vehicles had to be recalled. It was a big price to pay for the spiral of silence.

Darius Mehri, a former Toyota employee and author of a book about an American engineer's experience in Japan (*Notes from Toyota-land,* Cornell University Press, 2005), deplored the much celebrated *kaizen* technique as being 'driven by a fanatical emphasis on increasing market share'. He spoke about how heavily overworked the Japanese engineers were and that 'it was too hard for engineers to produce products without design flaws and too easy for managers to hide those flaws'. [4]

Bob Miesionczek, who had lived in Japan for many years and used to consult with Japanese multinational companies, felt that 'it is hard to divine the truth on the Toyota situation given all the politics involved. If Toyota knew about the serious safety issues and kept quiet, it would seriously violate all the core precepts of the Toyota philosophy.'

The Japanese management guru Sensi Masaaki Imai expressed a more benign view that 'the recall of Toyota vehicles shows the company's strength, not its weakness'.

An Indian commentator, Jerry Rao, was quite sure that Toyota would come out of its troubles because 'Any company led by a CEO, who is willing to unequivocally accept a mistake, publicly bow in contrition and emphatically apologize to customers who trusted the company, is a company with a future.'

Escaping the Spiral of Silence

The practical issue that a manager faces is to figure out what he can do to escape the ambiguity that silence produces. The spiral of silence may be due to the superior and it is important to reflect on whether the superior could be the cause of such behaviour.

The superior's body language may not be communicating that the superior wishes to hear about things more openly. I think that in at least half the situations, the superior is the cause. In that case, the superior needs to either change his own attitude or learn to cope with the situation that he has created. He has to find informal methods of connecting with the people in the organization.

It could also be the junior employee feeling far removed from the boss. Only the subordinate can overcome this feeling of distance. Expressing differences is a skill that the manager has to learn. A good way is to reflect on how the employee might like a message to be sent to him if someone below him had to communicate. Another way is to see if a solution can be offered rather than merely pointing out a problem.

Ignoring the difference is a short-term option, but doing so too long can produce unintended consequences. A CEO narrated one of his experiences to me.

Maria was supervising a department in an important institution in the company for over ten years. The department somehow had a huge churn of staff. In ten years, it saw about twenty changes at the leadership and operational levels.

Every staff member left citing a general reason for leaving. No precise reason for the attrition emerged. The problem could have been inadequate exit interviews or because the departing staff member wanted to go quietly. The issue of whether the department was being properly supervised by Maria came up occasionally at the senior leadership discussions, but the CEO found it difficult to tackle the matter directly. He did make some attempts, but he was not too direct in case such a conversation upset Maria. So there were two spirals of silence: one by the departing staff members and one between the boss and Maria.

After this long spiral of silence and skirting of issues, a crisis developed. A new staff member decided to speak up. He explained to the leadership that he could not continue working in the atmosphere that prevailed in the department and placed the problem squarely with the way the department was being supervised. Now the cat was out of the bag and the matter had to be addressed. Maria did not like it, but she accepted the responsibility and gave up her supervision of the department in the larger interests of the organization.

The CEO often reflected whether the issue could have been tackled without the crisis. When the CEO once broached the subject Maria had stormed out of the room. That made the boss cautious. Need he have been so hesitant to discuss the subject merely because it would upset Maria? He was sure that if he had applied his mind to it, he could have broken the spiral of silence. He regretted that he had not done so.

Box 8.4
KEY MESSAGES

It is human nature to assume that your interpersonal relationships are superior to others' relationships. This is a flawed view.

The spiral of silence and not expressing one's real views on a matter is not an infliction by other people. Your own ability to contribute to the spiral of silence is high.

If you assess that you are unable to thrive in an open atmosphere of expressing differences, then you either try to change or learn to listen to the song behind the words.

If you can change, then a cycle of positive actions can result.

See if a solution can be offered rather than merely pointing out a problem.

You can learn to promote a positive climate to avoid the syndrome of communicating 'yes' when you mean 'no'.

CHAPTER 9

Misconnecting
Saying What You Don't Mean

'Leadership failure is a behavioral phenomenon. Leaders fail because of who they are and how they act in certain situations.'
—Ram Charan

'Strange is our situation here on Earth. Each of us comes for a short visit, not knowing why, yet sometimes seeming to divine a purpose. From the standpoint of daily life, however, there is one thing we do know: that man is here for the sake of other men.'—Albert Einstein

In the previous chapter, the focus was on the importance of connecting with your workmates. You need to say what you mean, to say 'yes' or 'no' unambiguously on an issue, to speak up constructively when you have something to say and to ensure that an atmosphere is created where openness is prized.

This chapter deals with the flip side. You get misconnected with your people by inadvertently communicating messages in a non-verbal way. You may not mean what your non-verbal message conveys, but that is the message the recipient gets. So far as he is concerned, that is what you have 'said'.

The Bonsai Trap

In simple terms a bonsai trap is an inherent behavioural weakness which shows up in the way you conduct yourself. This is sometimes referred to as a 'derailer' or the 'dark side', though I rather like the term 'bonsai trap'. Over the years, the Center for Creative Leadership, North Carolina, has done some original work on 'derailment'. [1]

Bonsai-trapped executives are those who have earned recognition and promotion up to a certain level. After that stage, they find that they are on a plateau or, in some cases, even demoted or fired. Such leaders unknowingly diminish their ability to execute the tasks on hand. Hence there is the prevalent view that a successful leader must not only develop skills and strengths, but must also learn to manage his bonsai traps. Managing your negative impulses is quite important for success.

As evidenced by research, the most common bonsai trap is an inability to relate to people in meaningful ways. Executives who are perceived by their peers as being unable to develop strong interpersonal relations are described through one or more of the bonsai traps such as insensitive, competitive, self-isolating, dictatorial, overly critical, over-demanding, easily angered, arrogant, emotionally explosive, manipulative and aloof.

Unable to Climb out of the Bonsai Trap: Mithun's Story

Mithun had a fine academic record and an outstanding career. Then his bonsai traps derailed him.

His father was an outstanding professional manager, so Mithun was a second generation professional manager. This was not at all common in the days when Mithun began his career.

He graduated from an internationally acclaimed engineering college, worked in a multinational company for some time and then returned to India during the heady days when India's future in manufacturing was being built through new factories and modern infrastructure.

Mithun joined his first employer as a young engineer. He was bright, well educated, highly skilled and ambitious. The talent management spotlight in the company focused on these qualities. He secured rapid promotions and was appointed the company CEO in his early forties.

Mithun was bright, and he was deeply conscious that he was bright. Gradually and inadvertently, he displayed a superiority complex in his relationships with colleagues—what others perceived as arrogance. He was deeply aware of his father's reputation as an outstanding leader and perhaps that was why he resented being connected or compared with his father.

Mithun was well-spoken and articulate, but he was a loner and a bit aloof. He certainly was not the gregarious, backslapping archetype of a team leader. You could respect his intellect but you could not love the human being! He was perceived as being moody. His subordinates would try to gauge his 'mood of the day' while preparing for meetings with him. He was intensely proud of his company and his own accomplishments, not without reason. His pride made him resistant to any ideas for improvement. He knew what was best and nobody knew more than he did!

It is important to note that Mithun never said these things and never articulated such ideas. However, many people who worked with him thought of him as an aloof, stuck-up leader. Interestingly, this was the view of his subordinates, peers as well as superiors. He developed a particularly bad relationship with the directors of his company when he was at the helm.

India opened its economy in the 1990s and lowered import tariff rates. Foreign competition was threatening the cost structure of several industrial companies that had become 'great companies' in the old licence permit Raj. Mithun was caught up in a board debate on whether his company was doing enough as a response to the changing competitive environment.

The directors were unhappy for several reasons. Mithun was not forthcoming about the company's performance. He was reluctant to share any information with the directors and tended to be proprietary and secretive. He was convinced that his company was world class in efficiency, but he resisted evidencing that to the board. Unfortunately his company performance declined and showed a loss for the first time. The directors felt that they had to act. They made a change in leadership.

Mithun literally walked out with the attitude of 'Let me see how the company runs without me.' In reality, the company recovered and prospered, but he ended up walking into the abyss of anonymity. Mithun was derailed in his career; he was derailed in the quagmire of his bonsai traps.

It was not that he fell into his bonsai traps. Rather, he could not climb out of them.

Able to Climb out of the Bonsai Trap: Rustom's Story

Rustom was an entrepreneurial, solidly professional leader. He combined in a rare way the skills of a technologist with managerial abilities and a way of imagining a future for his business. Through his professional performance and persuasive articulation, he grew steadily in his international company. He was posted to head a country unit as part of his development and work experience.

As the country head, Rustom needed to integrate the eight top leaders' functional skills into a vibrant, results-delivering performance. His colleagues knew more about their own functions than Rustom did—about local customers, about finance, about relationships and so on.

Such a general manager must enter his new role with the genuine belief that he is surrounded by managers who are competent in their own functions. The only value addition that he had to do was to integrate the efforts of competent people, like the conductor of an orchestra. Rustom understood this in his mind. However, his behaviour did not reflect it, according to his team.

After about eighteen months, Gordon, the boss at the headquarters, thought he heard rumblings of dissatisfaction. Such reports from far off places pose a difficulty for the boss. He cannot fly down each time he hears something as it will disturb the equilibrium in the national company. The boss at HQ is supposed to have spent time and effort selecting the new country leader. Having done so, HQ bosses are supposed to leave the new leader to get ahead with the agreed tasks.

Initially, Gordon ignored the signal. At one point, Gordon's intuition told him that it was no more a signal, it was a message. The transition of a signal to a weak message, and the weak message to a clear message is a very important part of managing from remote locations. Gordon decided to spend a couple of days with the national company. However, unlike the usual PowerPoint presentations, field visits and dinner meetings with managers, Gordon asked to have one-on-one meetings with promising talent. This was not uncommon as the international company had a strong set of HR practices that encouraged such meetings.

During the thirty- to forty-five-minute meetings, Gordon picked up clear signals that there was indeed a great deal of unhappiness. The source of unhappiness was Rustom's behaviour. He was perceived as being mercurial and moody.

He would hurt senior colleagues in the presence of others. He was obsessed with his own image and came through as egoistic. 'He lives in his own I . . . I . . . I world,' as one colleague put it bluntly during his conversation with Gordon. However, all of those who spoke were unanimous, directly or tangentially, in praising Rustom's skills and strengths. They all pointed out that though there were instances of unacceptable behaviour by Rustom, Gordon should not lose sight of his tremendous value to the organization.

At the end of his visit, Gordon was quite uncertain about the course of action that he should adopt. He was puzzled. He was a foreigner. He was deeply conscious that there could be some local cultural angle, including some organizational politics. On the other hand, Gordon received messages of strong praise for several of Rustom's strong points, his positive and energizing attitude, his persuasive way with customers, and above all, his deep commitment to the vision of the company and its people.

So it was unlikely that some small group was trying to fix Rustom. On the other hand, there seemed to be an equally vehement negative reaction to the bonsai traps which Rustom was exhibiting. The implicit plea was to correct Rustom, but not to reduce his motivation or fire him. How should Gordon go about correcting a leader who was in his late forties?

After consulting his confidante and adviser back in HQ, Gordon decided that he must engage with Rustom, direct with his message, but not in a damaging way. He decided to write up his observations and present the message as 'what he had heard'. His visit notes were well crafted. In his thirty years of management experience, Gordon had rarely torn up so many drafts as he finalized the words, the tenor and the meaning in his note.

Rustom was devastated when he read the note on what Gordon had heard. He wished to talk more about the subject with Gordon. Gordon was reassured that he had got his message across clearly, and now had a window through which he could help Rustom. They sat down over a few meetings and decided on a course of action. Rustom felt reassured that the 'medicine for the road ahead was not to cure some debilitating, life-threatening deficiency'. Gordon felt that he needed to let Rustom find his space and solution without becoming too intrusive or directive.

A coaching relationship developed between Rustom and Gordon rather than a boss–subordinate relationship. Some behavioural interventions were planned unobtrusively. The process worked well. It was not that Rustom was a completely different person; it was just that his subordinates saw their boss making a genuine attempt to modify some toxic aspects of his behaviour. They too reached out to him.

The credit goes more to Rustom than to Gordon. Rustom was the one who adopted the 'I want to change' attitude. Gordon merely facilitated the process and, to his credit, did not assume a judgemental role. For the next several months, there was steady improvement in the state of relationships. It was not that Rustom suddenly stopped being volatile in his moods or stopped displaying his egoistic tendencies. The magic was that when his bonsai traps manifested themselves, Rustom had the self-realization that he 'had blown it again'. Thanks to his self-awareness, he could do other things to neutralize the occasional blow-up. Self-awareness and partial change of behaviour did the magic.

Bonsai traps are not only about personal behavioural traits; they extend to the attitude and approach of the leader as described in the next section. In fact, even companies are

Box 9.1   Self-destructive Habits

Bell South chairman F. Duane Ackerman once asked Professor Jagdish Sheth, 'Why do good companies fail?' The professor took the question seriously and started archival research to identify companies that were great in their time and then faded away. He found that the habits acquired by the companies on their way up accounted for their inability to adapt later.

He also concluded that good companies can survive if they recognize and take steps to counter self-destructive habits developed by them. So companies too have bonsai traps! The self-destructive habits that Professor Sheth identified are:

- Denial: myth, ritual and orthodoxy
- Arrogance: pride before the fall
- Complacency: success breeds failure
- Competency dependency: curse of incumbency
- Competitive myopia: nearsighted view of competitors
- Territorial impulse: turf wars and culture conflicts
- Volume obsession: falling margins and rising costs

It does seem that companies have bonsai traps that are similar to those of leaders.

supposed to exhibit self-destructive habits[2] as suggested in Professor Jagdish Sheth's book (*see* Box 9.1).

Slipping on the Oil Slick

There are many stories of how the mighty and successful get cut off from reality. One person who has narrated his story through his memoirs is Lord John Browne, former chairman of British Petroleum (BP).[3]

John Browne was born in 1948 in Hamburg to Edmund, a British army officer, and Paula, a Hungarian woman who had survived Auschwitz. His father was a 'determined officer in the

Black Rats tank regiment'; his mother was a refugee from Transylvania, Romania. Her family had perished in Nazi camps. She was slated for extermination, but survived. Given all the circumstances, his upbringing could be considered to have been tough.

John studied physics and business and joined BP in 1966. He had a stunning career progression and twenty-nine years later, he was appointed the Group CEO. Twelve years later, in 2007, he stepped down from chairmanship amid considerable and unfortunate controversy. What might have been the factors behind his downfall?

He was obsessed with BP as the company was central to his life. He was single and, barring the bond with his mother, he had no other social space. These factors might have made him unemotional in his dealings with employees and also intolerant of any shortcomings in them. Browne admits his loneliness, 'I became increasingly aware of the all-consuming action of being at the helm of BP and the emptiness of my private life . . . I did not know how to leave . . . there always seemed to be something I wanted to follow through . . . it is bad reason for staying.'

He started to take decisions on his own even though they may have merited discussions and consensus. He has admitted in his book that his own arrogance and a culture of complacency in BP contributed to BP's failure to prevent a huge oil spill in Alaska. 'As a leader it is hard to find that delicate balance between confidence, humility and arrogance. You need confidence to make decisions, to keep moving the business forward . . . yet arrogance may cause you to make a decision before considering the range of possibilities,' he writes.

He was tough, cerebral and a workaholic, who spoke in soft, almost inaudible tones. During his monthly meetings, he grilled managers on every aspect of their work. Managers were scared of his penetrating assessment of their work and to speak up. On the subject of oil spills, he was completely confident about the leak detection systems. Yet the Alaska leak happened, causing him to reflect, 'I wish someone had challenged me and been brave enough to say "We need to ask more disagreeable questions". His closest aides were vying to succeed him and allowed themselves to be blinded by his stature.

John was even-tempered, always dapper and organized. He was so orderly that his office looked as though no work was going on there. He was coldly ruthless in dealing with BP's affairs. He was held in awe by his subordinates to the point of them being frightened by him. It is unlikely that Browne intended all this, but that was the way it was.

You can wonder whether there is anything unique about this case. The cases of most downfalls bear an uncanny resemblance to one other. This aspect has been the subject of study by academics.

Seven Deadly Habits

In 1997, Sydney Finkelstein, a professor at Tuck Business School, conducted interviews of 197 managers in forty companies that had experienced severe corporate failure.[4] From his research, he deduced that there are seven deadly personal qualities of bonsai-trapped company leaders:

1. They have an exaggerated concept of themselves and of their company dominating the environment. They overestimate the extent to which they control events and underestimate the role of chance and circumstance in their success. They

have an exaggerated self-image of their personal contribution to the company.

2. They do not draw the line between themselves and their company. They steer the company to take unwise and big risks with the shareholders' money merely because they perceive themselves as risk-takers. They cause the corporation to enter business lines which are their favourites or personal interests without enough consideration of whether it is good for the shareholders. The CEO of a large company is the closest thing to being the king of your country!

3. They behave as though they have all the answers. They see several top-level colleagues as those who pay lip service or as people who are undermining the efforts of the CEO. They start to cut out their senior team from the decision process. They 'want to get on with it' and gradually wish to control the whole activity through setting up a personal staff.

4. If a team member is not hundred per cent behind the leader, that member is out as far as the leader is concerned. Some leaders state explicitly or subtly display a body language of not wanting to hear dissenting views. Gradually colleagues prefer not to speak up, thus affecting the leader's effectiveness and the employees' motivation.

5. The leader develops sensitivity to the manner in which he is perceived in the public domain; gradually this sensitivity grows into a magnificent obsession. Many leaders are brazen about cultivating their image; a few are subtle about it. The leader may spend more time on image-building rather than on running his company.

6. They underestimate major obstacles. He may be the diehard optimist who believes that obstacles will fade if only

managers persist. He may be the super-techie, who thinks that he knows the answer to everything technical. He may be hesitant to accept the weaknesses of his decisions, and will persist in his chosen path so that he is not seen as admitting his error.

7. They cease to invite new approaches to solving problems. They stubbornly rely on their own past experiences.

In short, these seven habits point to a style which becomes inward-looking, a style which leads to miscommunication with colleagues and team members.

Box 9.2
KEY MESSAGES

Every person has a repertoire of personal and behavioural weaknesses. These weaknesses cannot be eliminated; it may be possible to control them. These are called bonsai traps.

Becoming self-aware of these bonsai traps and adapting one's behaviour to reduce the manifestation of bonsai traps are immensely helpful. If you are unable to do this, you may not be able to escape from the bonsai traps.

Being aware, seeking help to mitigate the effects of your bonsai traps, displaying an open attitude and showing a willingness to adapt go a long way in helping you climb out of your bonsai traps.

There are certain types of 'toxic' behaviour that leaders tend to display. These types of behaviour can be recognized and curbed.

CHAPTER 10

Engaging
Without Hierarchy or Authority

'Let each become all that he was created capable of being.'
—Thomas Carlyle

I n this section of the book, we have been exploring the second of the three-world model, the world of people.

Chapter 8 was about connecting with people by saying what you mean, by seeking a way to express your positive or negative view on a subject in a constructive way. Otherwise the spiral of silence can create undesirable consequences and result in what we loosely refer to as 'office politics'.

Chapter 9 was about misconnecting with people by saying things that you do not mean. Our subordinates, peers and bosses do not merely listen to our verbal expressions. They perhaps pay more attention to our non-verbal signals than to what we say. The messages in our non-verbal signals are usually accurate; most likely, however, we never intend to communicate those signals.

This chapter explores the nature of the manager's engagement with his work. Professional managers are wired to expect clear lines of authority and accountability. Organization charts, job descriptions, reporting relationships and support services become so important that the manager becomes a slave to them; this means that he is unable to function without these appurtenances. This can be a handicap in entrepreneurial ventures or in senior organizational positions.

A leader's career path has three typical phases during which the executive learns to solve known problems with known solutions to solving unknown problems with unknown solutions. In late career he transits into relationships where there is no hierarchy or authority.

Change in Relationships and Engagement

There are two models to understand the shifting relationships as you progress through your career—the first is the 'escalator' model and the second is the 'concentric circles' model. Both have a similar message.

The Escalator Model

In the escalator model, during the early stages of the career, the inexperienced executive is expected to use relationships to solve known problems which have known solutions. For example, he may be assigned to run a limited sales territory or a production shop floor. The issues encountered in such a role are well known and so are the solutions. The idea is for the young person to learn the ropes of the manager's role, which is to work through other people.

He then steps on to the next escalator where he may be assigned to solve known problems with unknown solutions or unknown problems with known solutions: for example, to solve a long-standing problem of a difficult distributor or a labour union issue, entering a new export market or getting the best out of a team of older managers.

In the late stage escalator, the executive finds himself addressing unknown problems with unknown solutions: for example, taking responsibility for a strategic business unit but where all the business functions do not report to him or integrating the business plans of a number of business units into a cohesive whole or figuring out a new business model to enter a blue oceans market space.

The Concentric Circles Model

In the concentric circles model, you view this progression by observing the extent of control he has over the resources he needs to deliver results.[1]

In the innermost circle, he has almost full control over the needed resources and clear results to deliver: for example, to complete the sales targets every quarter.

In the next circle, he has clear results to deliver but lack of complete control over the required resources: for example, he has to get work done and seek cooperation from the whole organization. He has to use his influence and advocacy skills to accomplish the tasks.

In the outermost circle, he has to deliver with very little control over the resources that are needed to accomplish the task. He has to rely almost solely on advocacy and influence, for example, when he has to engage with a sovereign government to get permission to invest in the country or to save an existing investment.

The terms on which the executive engages with his tasks thus change throughout his career as he moves from certainties to uncertainties. An important part of learning what is not taught is to develop the adaptability to work without hierarchy or authority. This is the subject of this chapter.

These models might appear as though the transition occurs over a long period of time; however, this may not be so. Outlined below are three cases.

First is a person who cannot bear to be a professional manager and opts to start an entrepreneurial venture. He finds himself thrown into unknown 'unknowns' early on. The story of Kumar illustrates this situation.

Second is a manager who has worked in blue chip multinational companies and then joins an Indian business house in a senior position. Typically MNCs have a clearly defined organization chart, job descriptions and defined lines of authority and responsibility. They are very process oriented. Indian houses tend to be more flexible and fuzzy in these respects. 'Who matters' counts a lot more in Indian business houses than in MNCs.

Third is the story of a talented manager who found that being president of his building society was an unexpected challenge.

Kumar the Entrepreneur

The story of Kumar illustrates the dilemmas that arise from choosing an off-the-track path. Today, in his forties, Kumar is a successful freelance film writer, who has established a company to produce and direct feature films.

Kumar is a common bloke, the son of a retired judge. He has a sister and two brothers. Coming from a middle-class professional family, Kumar was constantly encouraged to study hard, qualify to join some profession and secure a job with a steady income. The elder sister and brother did just that. But young Kumar was different and restless.

He would study hard enough to pass and secure the approval of his father. He graduated in commerce and even completed his articles for chartered accountancy with a top-notch accounting firm. He did everything the way his parents had wanted. Although he studied diligently, he just could not see himself as a professional accountant. It was not in his dreams; it was not a door he even wanted to knock on. He felt that he would be trapped by systems and organizational constraints rather than be 'free to fly'.

Deep within, Kumar felt the passion for a career in films, something quite offbeat for a middle-class man. He loved watching Hindi films, and wanted to be a part of that world.

When he saw Rajesh Khanna acting in *Anand*, he fantasized himself in that role. When he read Javed Akhtar's scripts, he imagined himself writing scripts. He indulged himself in his passions, quietly and privately, perhaps assuring himself that he had the talent.

For Kumar, films were fun. Success meant doing the best with what he had. So how could he not be successful? He could see only one way forward.

At twenty-five, he announced to his family that he wanted to be in films. His father was aghast. He was sure that the young lad would dabble in it for a while and come running right back to join some firm as an accountant.

Kumar, BCom, ACA, started a theatre group, which allowed him to write scripts, act and direct plays. He virtually quit the world of commerce to have his idea of fun. It took seven years of struggle, but Kumar could not see any other way to lead his life. He was lost in the world he had created around himself; he enjoyed every moment.

He could be choosy about which roles he would accept because his family supported him. If his family did not support him, he would have accepted some lesser roles. Thus the family support accelerated his entry into films, but it was he who created an alternative path for himself. He had only one clear path forward, with no alternatives!

By the time he was in his late twenties, his family saw clear evidence of success. Kumar had acted in a television serial called *Subah*, which turned out to be a commercial success. After that, there was no looking back. He is happy that he was single-minded about his passion, but he ensured that he developed the talent to be successful.

The story illustrates how compelling the case is for the person concerned. Kumar's background encouraged him to qualify professionally and do what his father wanted him to do, that is, work and rise as an accountant. Why would a person like Kumar jump into the insecurity of the unknown or the outer circle? He mentioned the following reasons:

Inner voice and passion

Kumar had a calling, an inner voice that nudged him every day. Although the territory that he wanted to enter would be new, he was not daunted; rather its newness attracted him. It is the same reason why an explorer prefers a compass to a map. Kumar was being positively drawn to a film career.

Stifling professional prospects

Simultaneously he was being ejected from the world of accountancy by an intense dislike of doing that kind of work. He told me, 'I studied accountancy diligently, partly to satisfy my father, but also to be able to speak confidently about why I wished to avoid that career. The idea of being boxed into a company was quite unexciting for me.'

Opportunity to network

Kumar was a gregarious person. He loved building relationships purely for the heck of it. He was not a hierarchy-driven person. He built relationship networks because he thought they were good to build, not because some person could be useful to him later. Such people are referred to by Malcolm Gladwell as 'connectors' in *The Tipping Point*. They are the way they are because they are able to live in many cultures at the same time. Kumar was of that kind.

Making a difference

Kumar was confident that if you really enjoy Hindi movies, you could find some way of making a living out of your love. He knew he could make a difference. In spite of his self-confidence, if he faced failure, he could always get back to being an accountant.

Kumar seemed to embody all that is implied in the following quotation by Calvin Coolidge: 'Nothing in the world can take the place of persistence. Talents will not: nothing is more common than unsuccessful men with talent. Genius will not: unrewarded genius is almost a proverb. Persistence and determination alone are omnipotent.'

Madhav's Switch from MNCs

Madhav had enjoyed a successful career in three multinational companies, all of them well-known, blue chip companies with a positive image. During these twenty-five years, he had acquired extensive domestic and international experience in his field. He was a prized recruit as he prepared to join an Indian business house as a senior functional leader.

In general, you must assume that having a 'successful management education and experience' is like having a driving licence for many years. You know how to move the car. However, that does not mean that you can drive in any city in the world. Each city has its own rules and practices, and familiarity with streets is crucial.

In the same way, a manager joining a new company has to figure out the 'driving conditions and conventions' in that company. It is inevitable that a new manager will have the same lump in his throat during the first year as a first-time driver in Los Angeles sitting in a rental car would have.

Madhav joined the new company with a very different mindset: that he was a 'proven and accomplished' manager. According to him, that was why he had been recruited. He would help transform the Indian company by introducing MNC practices, which he believed were the way to salvation.

Madhav thought that the Indian company was a nest of intrigue and politics. He felt that leaders did not behave according to their titles or business cards. Some seemed to have more power than others. He sensed that many could say 'no' to him without putting an alternative on the table.

Nobody in the Indian company thought that he needed such salvation. The managers there had run their business successfully for several decades. They welcomed new blood to refresh the thinking, but not an arrogant person who thought his role was 'to teach them'. The consequences are not difficult to imagine.

Madhav lasted under twelve months. Although he had a valid driving licence, he could not drive his car in a new city largely because of his arrogance and his unwillingness to understand the core group, that is, who really mattered in the new company.[2]

Every company is run by a core group, the people who really matter. They may or may not be at the top table. The core group provides the drive and energy to the organization. The members of the group are the centre of the informal network in the organization. The power of the core group is derived from legitimacy, not authority.

To maintain success at senior levels, a leader must understand the existence of the core group, who really matters and how to work within that reality.

Girish the Building Association President

Girish was a prominent business leader in his city. His breadth of experience and knowledge was widely recognized. He moved to a new city as a routine part of his career. The family found 'the perfect house' in the new city, a three-storeyed charming old building with only seven residents and a small, family-like atmosphere.

The walls had Italian marble tiles, the staircases were wooden and there was enough parking within the building compound, a luxury in that city.

Within three years of Girish's moving in, he realized a number of truths. First, the six other residents had been there for several years. Second, they had fought with each other many times on many subjects. Third, they were virtually not on speaking terms with one another due to accumulated differences. Fourth, what came as a shock was that they all agreed on only one thing, that Girish should be the new president of the association.

Everybody must take turns at managing the association, his neighbours argued. Girish's sense of fairness and equity accepted that point of view. The residents argued that Girish could bring to bear his leadership and relationship skills and, for sure, everybody would listen to him. In a moment of weakness and misjudgement, Girish acquiesced. The world around Girish changed forever.

He found that this small association was a madhouse. Every member felt free to complain, but nobody felt obliged to put forward a solution. Any member felt that he or she could call him at any time of the day or night and on the most inconsequential of issues: 'the person upstairs is doing some repair work which is disturbing me' or 'the person downstairs has cluttered the landing with some works of art' and so on.

He was called by the lofty title of President, but his decisions could be called into question. Once he agreed that the mangoes hanging on the tree be cut and distributed to the residents. One neighbour was incensed because they had not agreed upon the manner of distribution. On another occasion, the sweeper wanted an emergency loan equivalent to four months' pay to meet a domestic commitment. How could the president agree without consulting?

It went on and on. Girish tried to put order by revising the by-laws, establishing a schedule of authority, planning in advance for members' meetings and all those sort of things that worked in his office environment. Each of them was a Herculean effort. Girish lost his patience and quit his post.

As he reflected on what happened, he kept asking himself why it was that he could operate in his corporate job, deciding on hundreds of crores of rupees, but got tripped in a small association. Initially, he thought it was to do with lack of systems and processes. Remedying that did not help. He then thought it had to do with cultivating everybody. Putting on the act of the friendly and helpful neighbour was exhausting and that too after a long, stressful day.

Finally the penny dropped. He had been trained to operate within his circle of control, but not much outside where he needed to rely solely on advocacy and influence. But as president of the building association, he had to work in the outermost circle. In this circle, he had to learn to operate without hierarchy or authority. He had to operate without any control of the resources. He had to relearn the skills of influence and advocacy for which he just did not have the patience.

This is the single reason why so often successful company leaders do not succeed in politics or public life. They do not know how to operate outside the first two circles.

PART IV

THE WORLD OF GETTING THINGS DONE

CHAPTER 11

The Architect and the Engineer
Imagining and Doing

This last section relates to the 'world of getting things done'. Implicit in this statement is that it is not about doing things yourself, but about getting things done by other people. This is an important distinction. I have seen very senior people who will take over the task and do it themselves rather than get it done by teaching subordinates how to do things.

One of the major barriers to turning knowledge into action is the tendency to treat *talking* about something as equivalent to *doing* something about it. A leader's task has two distinct dimensions. The first is the architectural dimension and the second is the engineering dimension. At higher levels, the former becomes quite crucial to success, while the engineering dimension increases in importance as you work in more junior roles.

The Architectural Dimension: Dilip

This dimension refers to the capacity of the leader to imagine shapes and events that are not palpable or obvious. It is about seeing what is not visible, hearing what is not audible and sensing future possibilities. It is the visionary role of the leader.

He conceives of how things may be in the future or how his company might be in the next three decades.

A top-level leader has to possess this capacity to envision and, more importantly, he should be able to communicate his vision to his team. It is this capacity that can energize his people to aim for big, hairy and audacious goals.

Dilip was a senior leader. He was very talented. He had qualified as an engineer and had a management degree too. By nature he was a curious person with a keen desire to learn about new things and think up new solutions to problems that he encountered. In other words, he 'enjoyed his innate restlessness'.

He began his career at a well-known engineering company. He displayed his technical curiosity and he also had great commercial instinct and could smell money in ideas. Such a combination in any young manager is bound to attract the attention of leaders. The CEO of his company selected him to work as his personal assistant.

Dilip was thrilled. That his CEO had picked him up appealed to him for two reasons: the first was the understandable reason that he had caught the attention of the seniors and the second was his implicit predilection to work with senior people, perhaps for reasons of power. His explicit and stated reason was that such exposure would give him a helicopter view.

For the next decade and more, he worked as the CEO's personal assistant. As he had expected, he got fantastic exposure. He cultivated the international business acquaintances of his boss; he interacted with the top leadership of his own company and the Indian competitor firms. He learned a lot. His capacity to imagine and dream developed rapidly. He started to develop an independent vision about the future of the business.

Within his current firm, his original mentor had moved on and there were several leadership changes. He also began to feel that he could not give wing to his dreams in the altered environment of his current employer.

He had got to know the charismatic managing director of Newco, another firm, as part of his network. He approached the managing director with the proposal that he would like to work in his firm. What would he like to do? He expressed a strong desire to work as his personal assistant. After thought and considerable persuasion, the managing director relented. Dilip joined the new firm.

Dilip spent the first five years in this new firm doing ad hoc projects for the managing director. He upset a number of people while settling into his new role. In the old firm, he had joined as a young person and, over a long period, he basked in the penumbra of authority and power of his forceful boss. After the boss's departure, Dilip felt a little disempowered.

In the new firm, it was different. He had joined at a senior level and had no starting 'equity' of influence or power. Dilip used to have an intellectual style about him and he could speak authentically about his long-term vision and dreams for a future.

The managing director of Newco decided to send the forty-five-year-old engineer to start up an allied engineering business to implement the vision that they had been developing jointly. This was almost the first time that Dilip had to work through others during his long career. This world of getting things done was not a world in which he had much experience.

Over the next decade and a half, Dilip slowly created the business that he had architected with his managing director. It was far from an easy ride. The people who worked with him found him to be a visionary. Unfortunately, he was perceived to have very poor people skills.

He was essentially a loner who could not build lateral relations. He also had little time for those who did not agree with him. His departments suffered much attrition and instability of tenure. He was perceived as mercurial and unpredictable. He was good at imagining but his skills of execution and implementation were under test.

Engineering Dimension: Pheroz

The engineering dimension of the manager's role refers to defining the problem or issue, detailing the action needed, ensuring that all the actions fit into a coherent pattern and executing with timelines and discipline. It assumes that an architect's vision is already available (*see* Box 11.1). Somehow young people seem to view execution tasks as a lower-level activity than strategy and planning. This is an incorrect view.

Here the emphasis is all about doing things and getting things done. In the process there are bound to be conflicts of views and approaches. The engineer has to confront these frictional conflicts, actively resolve them and ensure that the locomotion of the tasks continues with the least loss of speed.

Box 11.1 Implementing a Vision

Born in 1859, Sir Dorab was put through the paces by his father. Lying on his deathbed in 1904, Jamsetji Tata implored his son to execute his dreams and thus multiply the group's wealth for the benefit of the community. What was said of Sir Dorab after his death in Germany on 3 June 1932?

The *Nature* of London, in an obituary dated 2 July 1932, stated that Jamsetjee Tata had '. . . bent his adventurous talent to three great enterprises: the establishment of an Institute of Science to prepare Indians for the direction of modern large-scale industries; the construction of iron and steel works as an essential link in the economic cycle; and the harnessing of the prolific rainfall of the Western Ghats to electric power stations to relieve the dependence of Bombay on far-distant coalfields.' Sir Dorab Tata was more 'an executor rather than creator' who 'set himself the filial task of completing his father's work'.

Before leaving India in April 1932, Sir Dorab had executed a trust for the charitable endowment he had created, estimated at more than 2,250,000 sterling pounds.

The Times of London observed: '... it was by his work in carrying out his father's conception of iron and steel manufacture on a large scale in India that Dorabji rendered the most conspicuous service to Indian development and, incidentally, to Allied victories in the Eastern theatres of war ...'

A prophetic article titled 'Training Our Competitors: Asia's Time Is Coming', appearing in the *South Wales Daily Post*, published from Swansea, on 4 June 1932 had it thus: '... An age-old industrial problem is recalled by the death of Sir Dorabji Tata, the head of the Indian iron, steel and tinplate business, now in indirect competition with Welsh products for the Indian market ... Was it wise for us to provide an indispensable aid in the commencement of a competitive industry in the Indian Empire?'

In Sir Dorab's birth centenary year in 1959, the *Free Press Journal* of Bombay stated: 'There is more than sentiment in the enthusiasm with which the birth centenary of Sir Dorab Tata is being celebrated today ... His is "constructive philanthropy" at its very best ... the finest approximation we have to the creative utilisation of wealth such has been accepted as a creed by the Rockefellers, Fords and Carnegies ... The light that Sir Dorab lit must shine on.'

From the standpoint of history, Sir Dorab Tata's skills in implementing his father's vision counts among the most valuable. As the *Nature* newspaper recalled, Sir Dorab described himself as 'The Last of His House' because of 'the painful truth that with his passing an end came to a family which played a great part in the industrial renaissance of India'.

Pheroz was an outstanding engineer. He had studied management in spite of being a solid techie. He had no intention of abandoning a technical career. He joined an engineering company.

Pheroz came from an engineer's family. His father and uncle had also been in the profession. His elder brother was a technologist of some accomplishment in another firm. The home environment must have placed a technical career above a general management career. Pheroz never felt tempted to abandon his background as many of his peers were doing at that time by joining banking or marketing.

Pheroz asked to work on the shop floor with people. He was assigned to departments like the tool room and assembly shop where real, live technical issues would crop up with regularity. Pheroz looked forward to confronting these problems. He would roll up his sleeves and stand alongside his men to find an economic solution to the problem.

Pheroz seemed to thrive on facing problems. He was no loner; his people loved him because he was not the kind who would leave any problem unsolved. He would guide his people, work alongside them and celebrate the successes with them. His subordinates thought of him as a very approachable person with whom they could have frank discussions. The rapid rise of Pheroz within the company did not distance him from his team. 'They are my boys,' he would say with transparent pride throughout his career.

Pheroz took each day as it came. He did not have the trappings of an intellectual. So his conversations were never about a future vision and shaping the future. Such ideas may have been sloshing in his mind but he seldom articulated them. His people did not associate him with vision etc.

After several years, when the time came to select a chief for his company, a debate arose on whether Pheroz had the required vision. He got an opportunity to play the role. However, the feeling continued that he was more of a doer than a thinker.

The MAFA Syndrome

Erstwhile colleagues of N. Vaghul, the legendary former chairman of ICICI, recall his jocular reference to what he termed the MAFA syndrome—'mistaking articulation for action'. This is an elegant mnemonic of a significant management issue. Glib talking has become rampant in management circles these days.

It is wonderful to have great thinkers, excellent articulators and solid doers all rolled into one. Such people can rise to the very top.

Most people however display variability in the combination of skills that they bring to the table. How do you tell one variety from the other? For example, Dilip was perceived as clearly strong on the architectural dimension, but less endowed on the engineering dimension. Pheroz was perceived the other way round. And it is good to remember that both are only perceptions.

The advent of PowerPoint charts has elevated articulation capability from merely aural to visual. Even ordinary ideas are transformed into impressive packages with PowerPoint charts. Consultancy firms have elevated the art to such a high level that they come in with a pack 100 charts, specially made by their 'chart department specialists'. It is ironic that quite often they will leave the 100-chart pack with the client with the advice that 'only charts 3, 11 and 39 are really important'.

Presentations are the bane of modern management. Increasingly, managers seem incapable of functioning without their laptops and PowerPoint charts. The old art of a conversation on a business subject seems to be fast vanishing— the kind where one person tables a concept or proposition and people speak about it with the thrust of point and counterpoint, with the hope that a better idea will emerge from the debate.

I recall how one consulting company made a slick presentation to the whole cabinet of ministers on their research into the subject of what India can do to eliminate poverty within ten years. It was a power-punched, analytically rigorous, fantastically articulated presentation that lasted for an hour. At the end, Prime Minister Vajpayee was reported to have said in Hindi, 'All this is fine, but how will we implement such ideas?' That was the last we heard about the presentation.

Mind of the Architect and Engineer

It is clear that while one must be watchful of the MAFA syndrome, the architectural and engineering dimensions are both important in the world of getting things done. What are these mindsets?

In an engaging generalist book, Daniel Pink has forecast a subtle shift in the mindset of future leaders.[1]

Three factors are quietly driving a huge change, according to Pink. These are well known and have been commented upon widely.

The first is the fact of abundance in western societies. Consumers have all that they want. Lately, they have been shifting from seeking material wants to seeking meaning in life.

The second is the rise of Asia where there is a surge of knowledge-hungry, prosperity-seeking young people. They yearn to improve their lot in life and can do all sorts of tasks at a fraction of the cost of their 'ageing, overpaid' counterparts in the west.

The third is the breakthrough in automation. Information of all kinds is available with far greater ease to every knowledge worker, thus changing forever the basic nature of job descriptions and tasks.

After the above exposition, he forecasts a tectonic shift in the evolution of the 'ages'. We have witnessed the agricultural age giving way to the industrial age, then to the knowledge age. Now human society is in transition to the conceptual age, according to a persuasive Pink.

In the conceptual age, the fulcrum of thinking will shift subtly from L (left) brain thinking to R (right) brain thinking. Their relative importance will change; the two brains will not per se become more or less important. Most managers are products of the L-brained approach: analytical, logical and reductionist.

What is the R-brained approach? Creative and empathetic rather than logical and rational. R-brained thinkers are more influenced by design, empathy, story, play, symphony and meaning, according to Pink, and he goes on to describe these terms in his book.

Howard Gardner is the ultimate thinker about the various human minds.[2] Reviewing his theories, I wrote in 2007:[3]

In *Multiple Intelligences*, published in 1993, Gardner posited his theory of Multiple Intelligence (MI), comprising seven autonomous intelligences. Five of these are of the cognitive type, such as logical, kinesthetic, musical etc. Two refer to forms of interpersonal intelligence, which Gardner says are 'not well understood, elusive to study, but immensely important.'

The seven intelligences are abstract threads from the looms of Gardner's mind, and are of limited use to the real-world manager. But in his latest book, Gardner weaves those threads into a whole fabric. The five minds for the future consist of three cognitive minds—disciplined, synthesizing, creating—and two minds that concern our relations with other human beings—respectful and ethical.

Insightful and sometimes dense, *Five Minds for the Future* nonetheless tempts the reader to return to, and reflect on, many passages throughout the book. One example, 'In studies of teams involved in cardiac surgery, Amy Edmondson and colleagues have documented that successful teamwork depends more on the management skills than [on] the technical expertise of their leaders.' Another example, 'The ultimate ethical stance encompasses both the workplace as well as the surrounding community . . . What do I owe others, and especially those who are less fortunate than I am?'

Discipline is defined as a distinctive way of thinking about the world, informed by facts and figures we can memorize. Facts are useful, argues Gardner; but experimentation with such knowledge must follow. As Plato remarked, 'Through education we need to help students find pleasure in what they have to learn.'

Like many other management scholars Gardner points out the growing complexity of the information age and the need for a synthesizing mind to knit into a coherent whole all the information that is available from different sources. Synthesis is hard because human beings tend to learn only what is needed in a specific context. We have evolved to survive in niches. That is why when a successful manager moves from one industry to another, he or she finds it difficult to transfer knowledge. This requires creativity. Young people demonstrate Gardner's creative mind better than older people do. We see this in science, where younger workers are more likely to achieve breakthroughs, while older ones typically do synthesis. That is because older people lack inexperience. As Freud once observed, 'When I was young, ideas came to me; as I age, I must go half way to meet them.'

Of the two interpersonal minds, the respectful mind underscores the essential importance of affinity among human beings. To Gardner, being respectful means accepting our differences, learning to live with them and to value the traditions and habits of people who are different from us.

This aspect is visible in multi-cultural societies like the US. India is an even more dramatic example: she is simultaneously heterogeneous, yet bound together as one.

The Sanskrit word 'Swikriti' literally means acceptance, that is, people are entitled to lead their lives without any attempt to judge or compare the quality or standing of one group with reference to another. This inclusive attitude inspired by Swikriti made it easier for India to accept the traditions of Christians, Jews, Parsis, Muslims and other 'migrants' when they settled in India.

The ethical mind answers questions such as 'What does it mean to be a citizen of my community?' My experience has been that it is easier for managers to carry out good work in organizations and institutions, which basically strive to be good.

For example, Tata is ultimately owned by charitable trusts. The group has an institution (not physical, but virtual) called the Tata Relief Committee. This is a non-functioning committee in normal times. When any national calamity strikes (like the Koyna earthquake in 1969 or the Asian tsunami in 2005), the TRC assembles itself autonomously. It collects money from Tata employees and companies and offers volunteering work in cooperation with the authorities, for instance, cooking food packets or rebuilding homes. Tata strives to be good, and that enables its managers to be good.

L and R Brain: The Execution Platform

The fact is that we do not use one or the other brain at any point of time. Our brain switches between the left and right hemispheres automatically and our decisions and actions are based on where the fulcrum of the balance lies.

The point being emphasized is that we must recognize that the two hemispheres of our brain do exist and have different functions. All that we can do by becoming aware is to develop habits and skills that freely allow migration between the hemispheres.

For example, we can seek diversity in the type of people we employ so that different perspectives can come to the table. Many Indian business houses recruit from the better management institutes, where the outgoing student profile is mostly engineers. Would the companies gain by recruiting people with a holistic view of the world like social studies graduates and language students? Most certainly in the future.

The bald fact is that if your engineering dimension is not well developed, which means you are not a doer, a person who can execute, then your business career may not progress. Execution is the 'entry ticket' to senior management. Thereafter, if you display the architectural dimension as well, you are likely to be seen as a person with a great deal of potential.

To be a doer, an execution-oriented manager, you must appreciate that execution is a discipline that is not taught, but one you have to learn.[4] It is a discipline, it has to be a key role of the company leaders and it has to be part of an organizational culture. The execution challenge has three core processes: the people process, the strategy process and the operations process.

The people process involves knowing your people and selecting them with care. The strategy process is about setting the strategic direction and making sure that everyone is aligned to that direction. The operations process is about regular reviews. It is not an interrogation but a Socratic dialogue when tough questions get asked and debated.

Box 11.2
KEY MESSAGES

The leader has two principal roles: architect and engineer. Both are important.

───

Early in the career, the engineer, namely, the execution role, is key. Later in the career, the architect's role becomes key.

───

Generally speaking, to be successful, an 'architect' should have a good sense as an 'engineer' but every 'engineer' may not become an 'architect'. There are, as always, exceptions.

───

Articulation (and presentations) should not be mistaken for action.

───

The left and right brains, the analytical and holistic and integrating brains, hold the key to these skills.

CHAPTER 12

The Transformer
Leading with Affection

'The test of a first-rate mind is the ability to hold two opposing thoughts at the same time and yet retaining the ability to function.'—F. Scott Fitzgerald

The relationship between politicians and the public has changed dramatically over the last half century. Britain's post-war prime minister, Clement Atlee, needed to be and appear to be austere. When asked whether he had something to say to the public, he said tersely, 'No.' When his rival predecessor and successor, Winston Churchill, was advised to 'keep his ears to the ground', he responded that the public would find it difficult to look up to leaders who were perceived to be in that position! Today's politicians will meet, shake hands, twitter and do just about anything to stay connected with the public.

Politics is different from management, of course, but to the extent that both are social systems, there is a connection. The styles and relationships between the 'people' and the 'rulers' have changed significantly over just a few decades. When I reflect on my career spanning four decades, it seems to me that the world of managing people has been rebalanced from a centralized, directive, leader-centred form to a self-empowered, participative, employee-centred style.

It was not uncommon to see the progress of the 'kiss up kick down' executive in the past. Such a person would be solicitous, even grovelling, with respect to his upward relationships, but directive and harsh in his downward relationships. Looking into the future, the prospect for such a leader seems doubtful.

The American tycoon typified by Harold Geneen, Al Chainsaw Dunlap and Neutron Jack adopted a method of leading people which may not work today. In the 1980s, FMC CEO Robert Nuslott had said, 'Leadership is demonstrated when the ability to inflict pain is confirmed.' The same words cannot be said today, that is for sure.

On the other hand, you hear leaders like Jimmy Wales, the founder of Wikipedia, who says, 'You can't tell people what to do. When the right people are deployed in the right ways, a lot of directives aren't necessary.' The time has surely come for a new type of leader—one who has cast aside his large ego and thinks and acts in a humane way.

The Humane Leader

In South Africa, when two people meet they exchange the greetings *sawu bona* and *sikhona*. The first greeting means 'I see you' and the reply is 'I am here.' Unlike many other societies where you invoke the almighty or seek nature's blessings in the way you greet each other, the South African version is recognition of the existence of the being. In Zulu, they speak of the 'spirit of Ubuntu' which means 'you bring me to life and existence'.

These are live expressions of recognizing, above all, a human being as a human being. You have to treat an employee like a human being, with affection, more than ever these days. One businessperson who is universally regarded as a transformer is the late J.R.D. Tata. In this chapter, I draw instances and lessons from Tata, particularly J.R.D. Tata's life and experiences.

A leader is a leader only when he is able to transform, when he is able to architect a plan *and* engineer its implementation. To accomplish this, he must be the quintessence of a transformer and possess the skills of a transformer.

Organizational leaders are of three varieties according to Julia Middleton.[1]

The first is the 'rebel' who advocates a point of view in such a manner that people whose opinion needs to be enlisted cease to take him seriously. Typically such a person articulates an opposition to another's point of view very persuasively but fails to place an alternative on the table. The audience likes to listen to such demagogues but does not take them seriously if what they say is 'Do not do this, but I have no practical suggestions either.'

The second is the 'idiot' who is a person with deep expertise in one area but has no appreciation or comprehension of the whole. Such a person is accorded a great deal of respect for his narrow expertise but is unable to contribute holistically, howsoever well-intentioned he may be. He is akin to the scientist or attorney who sits on a company board and can speak only when his area of expertise arrives or the highly skilled neuro-specialist who finds the chairmanship of the hospital board to be an administrative nuisance.

Transformers Care and Listen

The third and the most desirable is the 'transformer' who recognizes that transforming is an evolutionary process, often slow. He advocates a clear viewpoint, but his mind is open to new ideas. He persuades those who oppose as much as he seeks the support of those who agree. He is sensitive to different world views and even sublimes his own view to accommodate others' opinions. To accomplish all this and more, the transformer has to rely on others and cannot make loneliness a virtue.

Many able men have been lonely because they do not consult or share. Charles de Gaulle often said that he felt the 'chill of loneliness'. President Jimmy Carter titled his book about his White House years *Lonely*. Loneliness is an unfortunate part of the menu of leaders. But if only a leader could listen and consult, the burden of leadership seems to get considerably lighter.

J.R.D. Tata epitomized this virtue of listening (*see* Box 12.1). When asked what has been the driving force of his life, he said, 'Honestly if I had not been the son of RD Tata, one of the Tatas and the son of one of the main Tatas, I don't think I would have been so driven . . . I know that all my colleagues have their own views and on many views of theirs I do not agree and they don't agree perhaps with mine.'

Transformers Do What Is Right

When referring to kindness and affection as the qualities of transforming leaders of the future, it may seem that such leaders are too good for this world, that they are less effective because they are good natured; this is just not true. The affectionate or

Box 12.1   The Consultative Leader

J.R.D. Tata said:

'I had no training in management but when I started in 1926, some books on management were being written. Not having an academic training in engineering and technology, my only contribution to management had to be in handling men who had been so trained. Every man has his own way of doing things. To get the best out of them is to let them exploit their own instincts and only intervene when you think things are going wrong. Therefore all my management contributions were on the human aspect through inducing, convincing and encouraging the human being . . .

'One thing I regret is never having been in line management except in the airlines. As I had no technical training, I always liked to consult the experts. At times I felt like the soldier who has never been an officer catapulted to be a General. When I have to make a decision I feel I must first make sure that the superior knowledge of my advisors confirms the soundness of my decision; secondly, that they would execute my decision not reluctantly but being convinced about it; thirdly, I see myself in Tatas as the leader of a team, who has to weigh the impact of any decision on other Tata companies, on the unity of the group.'

Source: *The Joy of Achievement*, R.M. Lala, Penguin, 1995

kind leader does what needs to be done with fairness and firmness. It is important for him to figure out whom he owes his sense of fairness to.

The fraud at Tata Finance was an unfortunate case and it required the leadership to act with firmness and fairness (*see* Box 12.2). The victims of the fraud, the investors, certainly thought of the leadership as kind and affectionate precisely because they acted firmly and fairly to protect the interests of the investors.

Box 12.2 Grime and Salvation

What does a corporate house do when the managing director of one of its companies, who is respected and trusted, commits fraud? Does it try to put a lid on the affair, or does it make an all-out effort to ensure that stakeholders suffer no losses, initiate an extensive inquiry to find out what went wrong and where, take exemplary punitive action against those responsible and, finally, introduce changes in the system to prevent such problems from recurring?

When Tata Finance was engulfed in a financial mess, the Tatas took the latter course, setting new standards for corporate governance in India.

In April 2001, Tata Finance floated a rights issue of preference shares. The issue had already opened for subscription when a letter, dated April 12, 2001, written by someone who called himself Shankar Sharma, was sent to the directors of Tata Finance, to the Securities and Exchange Board of India (Sebi), the market regulator, and to major newspapers. The letter levelled several allegations against Tata Finance and its then managing director, Dilip Pendse, charging that there had been a fraud committed in the company and that the prospectus of the issue contained false information.

Bharat Vasani, general counsel, Tata Sons, recalls, 'The company management came out with an advertisement in the newspapers the next day, stating that the allegations made by Shankar Sharma were untrue.' Mr Vasani and other senior Tata executives soon discovered that they were hugely mistaken. 'That letter alerted us,' says Ishaat Hussain, finance director, Tata Sons, 'and further investigations revealed that there had indeed been some serious irregularities.'

The first reaction at the higher rungs was one of surprise, shock and dismay. 'We were all taken aback,' remembers Mr Hussain. Tata Sons Chairman Ratan Tata then laid down the principle by which the Tatas would deal with this matter in the days and months to come: get to the bottom of the affair and handle the consequences honestly and transparently.

By May 25, 2001, it was painfully clear that Tata Finance had become almost insolvent. Even though the exact nature of the problem was not clear, it was emerging that the company had lent more than Rs524 crore by way of intercorporate deposits to some of its own subsidiaries and affiliate companies, and a significant chunk of that money was used to deal in the stock market highly speculative scrips.

The Tata Finance board expressed loss of confidence in the managing director, Mr Pendse, and decided to initiate an investigation into the financial affairs of the company and its subsidiaries. That was but the first step in a comprehensive clean-up that would have a profound impact on the company and other Tata companies in the days ahead.

Rather than sweep the issue under the carpet, the Tatas decided on a two pronged course of action. First, the interests of the small depositors who had placed their trust in the Tata brand name had to be protected. Second, an open and objective inquiry would be conducted to bring the culprits to book.

'Mr Tata recommended to the Tata Sons board that they stand behind the company and make available funds to meet all its financial commitments,' says Mr Hussain, 'and the board fully endorsed this.'

This may sound simple, but the resources required for such an exercise were staggering. Of the Rs2,706-odd crore that Tata Finance held in deposits, about Rs875 crore were from over 4 lakh small depositors. Had there been a run on the institution, massive amounts of cash would be required to pay those looking to safeguard their savings.

Tata Sons and Tata Industries made available to Tata Finance cash and corporate guarantees amounting to Rs615 crore. On July 25, 2001, a public statement was made, admitting that Tata Finance was in distress as a result of fraud committed upon it, and that the Tatas would ensure that no depositor lost any money.

'We kept a special counter for depositors to redeem their deposits,' Mr Vasani recalls, 'but, to our utter surprise, very few decided to withdraw their money. There were some withdrawals, but these almost stopped when people realised that we were ready to refund their entire deposit for the asking. We even obliged those who wanted to make premature withdrawals.' Simultaneously, Kishor Chaukar, who was on the Tata Finance board, and Mr Hussain personally visited all the banks that had lent monies to Tata Finance to assure them that the Tatas would stand solidly and fulfil the obligations of the beleaguered company.

Interestingly, before the fraud could be detected by the regulators, it was the Tatas' self-disclosure that opened the matter up. 'Our top management team personally met the RBI governor and the Sebi chairman and explained the situation,' says Mr Vasani.

Tata Finance, through an internal team and external investigators, found that a large number of share market transactions were made to secure personal profits and that Mr Pendse had amassed huge amounts of money at the company's cost. Tata Finance discovered that he had purchased a large number of shares of three companies, Global Tele-Systems, DSQ and Vakrangee Software. And, in many instances, the counter parties were the former managing director's family members, friends and companies. The internal team and external investigators also evaluated available documents and built up a paper trail. In the first week of August, based on legal advice from an eminent criminal lawyer and a report from an independent chartered accountant, Tata Finance and Tata Industries filed an FIR (first information report) with the Economic Offences Wing, Mumbai Police, against Mr Pendse and certain former Tata Finance employees.

But matters were not to end here. 'We moved the courts when the Mumbai Police filed a closure report with respect to our complaints,' says Mr Hussain. 'We took the stance that we will not let go the culprits. We moved the Bombay High Court and got the investigation transferred to the Central Bureau of Investigation. In the Supreme Court, too, our stand was vindicated. Six criminal complaints were filed in all, including three with the Delhi Police, and six complaints with Sebi for violation of various securities laws.' Mr Pendse was charge-sheeted in two complaints and taken into judicial custody.

Despite the alacrity with which the Tatas moved against Mr Pendse and his accomplices, the public perception of the Tata brand was affected initially. 'I think that there was a huge amount of dismay among the public on how such a thing could happen in the Tatas,' says Mr Hussain. But the Tata's ethical handling of the scam prevented any lasting damage. 'Did it damage our credibility? I don't think it did, but it did damage our image for a while.'

Fact is, in the longer term, the handling of the Tata Finance saga has been a demonstration of the uprightness of the Tatas. 'Which industrialist would have put hundreds of crores into a company that was sinking, and that too without being sure that any of it could be recovered?' asks Mr Vasani. 'This was an unprecedented response and one that I have never ever heard of in my career.'

The adverse media reaction was a different kettle of fish. Mr Hussain felt that the circumstances surrounding the case were partly responsible for the Tatas' troubles on this front. 'At that time, it was very difficult to believe that just one person could have done it,' he says. 'There were all kinds of conspiracy theories doing the rounds. We did not have all the evidence in the early days. It was a very complex fraud; the investigation by the police was not moving as expected, though they had all the documents.'

'The people who were responsible for maintaining checks and balances could have blown the whistle. But apparently they chose to keep quiet,' says Mr Vasani.

The scandal led to a string of changes in the internal practices of Tata companies. The chief financial officers of Tata enterprises now have direct reporting line to Bombay House, the Tata headquarters in Mumbai, there is a written code to prevent insider trading.

There is a whistleblower policy to encourage employees to report concerns about people possibly or actually violating the Tata Code of Conduct. The idea is to support people like 'Shankar Sharma', whose letter led to Mr Pendse and his accomplices being exposed.

Who, by the way, was Shankar Sharma? 'We have not been able to identify this mysterious person,' says Mr Vasani, 'but he could be an insider. He possibly had the interest of the Tatas at heart, but maybe not the courage to come out openly and report the happenings.'

The Tatas have also demonstrated by their action that they will not tolerate violations of the Tata Code of Conduct, and that those who attempt to subvert this value system will be dealt with sternly, including having to face dismissal from their jobs and legal action.

Mr Hussain is certain that the structure of Tata companies has, in the final analysis, been strengthened by the Tata Finance fiasco. 'But we cannot be policemen; boards have to shoulder the responsibility. Having said that, there is far more accountability today with regard to the boards of our companies.'

Tata Finance, itself, has bounced back to health from the troubles it had to endure. The company returned to profitability in 2003–04. And what of the scandal? Says Mr Vasani: 'This is a unique instance in India's corporate history.

I see it becoming a case study in management schools to demonstrate how ethical behaviour is not merely the right thing to do, but also how such behaviour can work to enhance and protect a brand.'

The biggest area of business for Tata Finance was vehicle financing; this business was merged with Tata Motors in April 2005. Following the merger it was ensured that the stakeholders of Tata Finance, especially its employees and shareholders, were not penalised. The business continued under Tata Motors till September 2006, when it was carved out as a wholly owned subsidiary that is now called Tata Motors Finance. The company is registered as a non-deposit taking, non-banking financial company (NBFC).

Furthermore, the Tatas have made a renewed, stronger and more holistic foray into the financial services sector by setting up Tata Capital in September 2007. Tata Capital is a wholly-owned subsidiary of Tata Sons and is registered with the Reserve Bank of India as a 'systemically important non-deposit accepting NBFC'. The company aims to fulfil the diverse needs of retail and institutional customers in multiple areas of business, such as retail and corporate finance, investment banking and services, private equity and rural finance.

(Reproduced with permission from *Code of Honour*, ed. Christabelle Noronha, Westland, 2009)

Transformers Surround Themselves with Talent

A key challenge of the transformer is that he is surrounded with multiple and opposing views. The greater the transformation sought to be achieved, the greater the diversity of views. That is why the words of Scott Fitzgerald are so important: that a first-class mind means the ability to hold two opposite points of view in the mind simultaneously and yet be able to function.

Transformers surround themselves with top-class people. If they don't, then they do not even get the diverse points of view around the table. How can you choose the 'best' course of action if the options do not include the alternative 'good' courses of action?

J.R.D. Tata was deeply conscious of his lack of a technical education and his lack of academic preparation to lead Tata when he said:

> I hadn't really the training to run a big group . . . I decided that where Tata was concerned, we must bring in people, top people, wherever we could, realizing that every company should have professional management. So in that sense I was a believer long ago of the need for independent, professional management for every company. Others did not realize it but I did.

Transformers Have Inspiring Aims

Jamsetji Tata gave the House of Tatas its unique position in the country. His conduct shows that particularly in his later years Jamsetji did not seek to create the most profitable enterprises. His question seemed to be what does the nation need? J.R.D. Tata seemed to do likewise by often asking, 'What does India need?'

Alfred Sloan became famous for saying in a different era, 'What is good for General Motors is good for America.'

JRD seemed to think the other way around, 'What is good for India is good for Tatas.'

Transformers Patch Up Differences

Listening and consulting inevitably mean that some differences will always be there. If the boss has consulted many and taken a different course of action from the one suggested by a person, he is likely to feel ignored. Ignoring some colleagues is inevitable when the boss has to choose from opposite viewpoints. However, transforming leaders allow differences but do not let them linger or persist. They patch up so that the difference is an anecdote of history, much like a husband and a wife do periodically.

An incident involving a heated exchange between J.R.D. Tata and a senior Tata director, A.D. Shroff, threatened the continuation of Shroff's association with Tata. Shroff sent his resignation. The matter was patched up by JRD with a great sense of egalitarianism and humility:[2]

Letter dated 23 August 1951 from J.R.D. Tata to A.D. Shroff:

I was surprised and upset at receiving your letter. I do not remember exactly the words I used during the somewhat heated exchange at the agents' meeting but my complaint to you was merely that an argument you used to score a debating point over me was not an honest one. That is surely a far cry from questioning your honesty and I am surprised that you interpreted it in that way.

You have a right to resent my speaking angrily or showing you discourtesy as a result, and for that I sincerely apologize, but if friends and associates decided to part every time they had an argument, life would become very difficult.

You refer to my firm. Except that I am personally a relatively minor shareholder, I don't think there is any difference on that account in any of us. We all work for it and we should think of it as <u>our</u> firm.

The trouble with both of us is that we both have a hell of a temper!

Transformers Have Empathy for People

The ability to experience another person's feelings is empathy. This is not easy as we all have different experiences and lenses through which we view events and life. A common company malady is that executives work late and insane hours, sometimes due to overwork but often due to keeping up with the Joneses. On the eve of J.R.D. Tata's sixty-fifth birthday in 1969, his secretary addressed the following memo to all his managing directors:[3]

> The chairman finds a continuing habit amongst various companies and departments in Bombay House to send for perusal/action a mass of papers every Friday afternoon. He appreciates the desire of officers to clear their desk before the weekend, but not the practice of compelling him to spend most of his weekend in clearing his! He has given his secretariat the orders that all but the most urgent papers sent to his office after 1 pm on Fridays should be sent back to the sender.

Once in 1944 JRD met Gandhiji along with two other business leaders.[4] As was the custom, Gandhiji's secretary,

Pyarelal, took notes of the meeting. After the meeting was over, JRD casually mentioned to Sarojini Naidu that he was a bit surprised that the private conversation was being noted and recorded. Gandhiji learned about the comment from Sarojini Naidu. He promptly had the notes destroyed and a suitable letter sent to JRD. JRD was extremely apologetic and wrote to Gandhiji, 'I am distressed to think that my remark, as conveyed to you, may have caused you some concern or hurt and that I was unwittingly responsible for the destruction of the record of the many valuable and thought-provoking things you said to us.'

Transformers Lead with Affection

J.R.D. Tata advocated an open communication among people in order to get the best out of relationships. He stated that the three most important requirements for getting along with people were: communication, total honesty and trust.[5] He also practised what he preached, as he told his biographer several years later:[6]

> When a number of persons are involved I am definitely a consensus man. But that does not mean that I do not express my views. But basically it is a question of having to deal with individual men heading different enterprises. And with each man I have my own way. I am one who will make full allowance for a man's character and idiosyncrasies. You have to adapt yourself to their ways and deal accordingly and draw out the best in each man . . . It may be that because all others were older than me when I became the chairman, I became a consensus man . . . If I have any merit, it is getting on with individuals in

their ways and characteristics. At times it involves suppressing yourself. It is painful but necessary . . . To be a leader, you have got to lead human beings with affection.

It is difficult to imagine that the head of such a large conglomerate would advocate suppressing himself and adapting to the way of his colleagues instead of what we see all around us, which is colleagues and subordinates adapting to the boss! Perhaps this is what it means to lead with affection.

Notes

Preface

1. *Crucibles of Leadership*, Robert J. Thomas, Harvard Business Press, 2008.
2. *The Leadership Engine*, Noel M. Tichy, Harper Business, 1997.

Chapter 2: The Framework of Three Worlds

1. *The Case of the Bonsai Manager*, Penguin, 2006.
2. *Lessons Leaders Learn*, TMTC, Pune, 2008.
3. *The Lessons of Experience*, Morgan McCall, Michael Lombardo, Ann Morrison, Free Press, 1988.
4. *Crucibles of Leadership*, Robert J. Thomas, Harvard University Press, 2008.

Chapter 3: Explicit Feedback

1. 'Unskilled and Unaware: How Difficulties in Recognizing One's Own Incompetence Lead to Inflated Self-assessments', Justin Kruger and David Dunning, *Journal of Personality and Social Psychology* 77(6): 1121–34.
2. *Indian Express*, 20 February 2010.
3. *Why CEOs Fail*, David Dotlich and Peter Cairo, Josey Bass, 2003.
4. 'Managing with the Brain in Mind', David Rock, *Strategy+Business* Autumn 2009.

Chapter 4: Implicit Feedback

1. *Elephant Bill*, J.H. Williams, Doubleday, 1950.
2. *When Elephants Weep*, Jeffrey Masson and Susan McCarthy, Vintage, 1994.
3. 'Holy Grail of Evolution', Natalie Angier, *International Herald Tribune*, 15 October 2009.
4. 'Lessons of Silence', Bruno Kahne, *Strategy+Business* 22 May 2008.

Chapter 5: The Physical Self

1. 'The Simplest Way to Reboot Your Brain', Robert Stickgold, *Harvard Business Review* October 2009.
2. 'Sleep Deficit: The Performance Killer', Charles A. Czeisler, *Harvard Business Review* October 2006.
3. 'New Year Irresolution', *The Economist* 2 January 2010. www.economist.com/procrastination
4. 'Be Like a River', Bharat Savur, *Hindu Business Line*, 11 December 2009.

Chapter 6: The Psychological Self

1. *The Tao of Physics*, Fritjof Capra, Fontana, 1976.
2. *The Road Less Traveled*, M. Scott Peck, Hutchison, 1983.
3. 'What Makes Us Happy', Joshua Wolf Shenk, *The Atlantic* June 2009.
4. 'A Basic Human Pleasure', Nicholas D. Kristof, *International Herald Tribune*, 18 January 2010.

Chapter 7: The Ethical and Spiritual Self

1. *Winners Never Cheat*, Jon M. Huntsman, Wharton School Publishing, 2006.
2. *The Courage to Act*, Merom Klein and Rod Napier, Magna Publishing, 2004.

Chapter 8: Connecting

1. *When You Say Yes but Mean No*, Leslie A. Perlow, Crown Business, New York, 2003.
2. Dhananjay Mahapatra, *Times of India*, 13 February 2010.
3. 'Secretive Corporate Culture Led Toyota Astray', *Wall Street Journal*, 13 February 2010.
4. 'Kaizen Goes Kaput', Darius Mehri, *International Herald Tribune*, 15 February 2010.

Chapter 9: Misconnecting

1. *CCL Guide to Leadership in Action*, edited by Martin Wilcox and Stephen Rush, Jossey-Bass, 2004.
2. *The Self-destructive Habits of Good Companies*, Jagdish Sheth, Pearson Education, 2007.
3. *Beyond Business*, John Browne, Weidenfeld and Nicolson, 2010.
4. *Why Smart Executives Fail*, Sydney Finkelstein, Portfolio Penguin, 2003.

Chapter 10: Engaging

1. *Beyond Authority: Leadership in a Changing World*, Julia Middleton, Palgrave Macmillan, 2007.
2. *Who Really Matters*, Art Kleiner, Currency Doubleday, 2003.

Chapter 11: The Architect and the Engineer

1. *A Whole New Mind*, Daniel H. Pink, Marshall Cavendish Business, 2008.
2. *Five Minds for the Future*, Howard Gardner, HBS Press, 2007.
3. 'An Appetite for Effectiveness', R. Gopalakrishnan, *Strategy+Business* Winter 2007.
4. *Execution*, Larry Bossidy and Ram Charan, Crown Business, 2002.

Chapter 12: The Transformer

1. *Beyond Authority: Leadership in a Changing World*, Julia Middleton, Palgrave Macmillan, 2007.
2. *A.D. Shroff*, Sucheta Dalal, Penguin, 2000.
3. *JRD Tata Letters*, Arvind Mambro, Rupa and Co., 2004.
4. *Beyond the Last Blue Mountain*, R.M. Lala, Penguin, 2003.
5. *Working and Growing Together*, Michael John Memorial Lecture, 1985.
6. *The Joy of Achievement*, R.M. Lala, Penguin, 1995.

Index